Dark Psychology Secrets Revealed

Mind The Gap Between Perception and Reality

MARK TEMPLE

Copyright © 2019 Mark Temple

TABLE OF CONTENTS

INTRODUCTION

Dark Psychology is a dark and complex subject.

It refers to the study of the human psyche as it delves into the psychology of what compels human beings to prey upon others.

Every human being on the planet has a dark side. Whether they are capable of causing a great degree of harm or mildly affect other people's lives depends on a lot of factors; the environment, the person's childhood, parental relationships, and more. However, the fact remains: every person is capable of dark deeds. Think that is a rather far-fetched statement to make?

Let us examine the dark side of human nature from another viewpoint.

Have you ever watched the news about people who go on to commit horrendous acts of violence? When interviewing the neighbors or family members of the perpetrators of such despicable acts, you might find people painting a rather vibrant picture. For example, in 2012, a 24-year old by the name of James Holmes killed 12 people during the screening of the movie *The Dark Knight Rises*. According to a high school acquaintance of the killer (Bankoff, 2012), James was "really smart" and "super nice kid".

But if Jams was indeed a "nice kid" as some people claimed, then why did he commit an act of unspeakable violence? What compelled him to "go over the edge," as the saying goes?

Turns out, nobody knows.

No psychologist can accurately predict whether someone is capable of dark actions. The mind is a mystery and psychologists have only scraped the tip of the mental iceberg. This brings us to the question: If we can't even predict what others are capable of, can we gauge the level of darkness that resides within us?

There was an interesting study conducted by a professor of psychology at the University of Texas-Austin (Goldhill, 2018). Professor David Buss was conducting research for his latest book. For it, he surveyed 5,000 to try and get a glimpse of the mind. His results?

95% of men and over 84% of women had dark thoughts.

More specifically, they had thought about killing someone. In numerous cases, these people often imagined a hypothetical victim and the *modus operandi* of the killing that they had in mind.

Pretty dark, isn't it?

But that's not all.

According to this report by the BBC (Petterle, 2009), we are all born violent. This is because until the age of three, we don't have any impulse control mechanisms. Three years after our birth, our prefrontal cortex begins to develop, allowing us to manage our aggression. The more this region develops, the better control we have over our darker reactions such as anger, envy, rage, and Narcissism, to name a few.

However, our dark side has an edge over the light.

If this was Star Wars, then the Sith army has a head start over the Jedi (which typically, they do). The only difference here is that the "Sith" part of our minds cannot be destroyed by finding a weak point, the way Luke did for the Death Star. We can only subdue it long enough for some of our better parts to surface and reveal itself to the world. But under the surface, the darkness remains.

This might seem like I am romanticizing the idea of our dark nature. But hardly. Research has proven that we respond more towards negative stimuli than positive ones.

Based on research conducted at Ohio State University by John Cacioppo Ph.D., participants were shown three different sets of pictures.

One set displayed positive objects that could arouse positive feelings, such as a pizza or a Ferrari. The second set featured objects such as a dead cat or a mutilated face, selected specifically to evoke negative feelings. The final set acted as a control group and featured images of objects like hair dryers and plates that were aimed to not generate either positive or negative feelings.

While the participants were examining each set of pictures, their cerebral cortex was being monitored. This area of the brain helps the researchers determine the degree of information passing through the brain.

The result? And you might have already guessed this.

Yes, indeed. It was discovered that the brain reacts strongly to negative stimuli.

Why are all these case studies and researches highlighted here?

To prove that Dark Psychology is a complex subject. While it does focus on the darker aspects of human personality, it does not reveal the motivations behind them. We are all capable of dark deeds. But for some of us, we only use them in defense, when we feel threatened. Those of us who know some psychological tricks often utilize them (sometimes without our knowledge) to gain some information, defend against psychological attacks, or simply protect ourselves in stressful mental situations.

When our ancestors used to live in caves, everything was clear-cut and simple. If someone showed aggression, then they would adopt one of two tactics; they would fight or they would flee. Most of the time, the opponent's actions were obvious. But as human beings evolved, so did our thought processes.

These days, everyone is capable of harboring layers of thought processes. Understanding people is not as easy as it was during the time of our ancestors.

However, with the growth in human understanding, beliefs, intelligence, and mental capabilities, there is also a growth in the perception of what the human mind is capable of and the reality of the capabilities of the human mind.

It is not farfetched to imagine that mental manipulations and mind control are possible. However, our notion of the two phenomena is based on Hollywood's interpretation of it. It always involves people wiggling their hands in front of someone's face and dominating their mind. Or perhaps swinging a pendulum in front of a person and asking them to submit to their will.

But the reality is far from it. Mental manipulations are not a result of psychic powers.

Think of the case against alleged cult leader Keith Raniere, who was charged on counts of sex trafficking (Berman, 2018). Many of the women who were rescued from his cult gave chilling records of how they were "empowered" by his cult. Some even chose to submit themselves to the cult's ideologies and beliefs.

Or why not take an example from everyday life. Do you know about the placebo effect? It is a psychological phenomenon that is common during medical trials. In essence, a placebo is a substance that has no beneficial effect on the body. During pharmaceutical or medical trials, people have been known to be given placebos (like a sugar pill) and told that they had just ingested a new type of anxiety relief medicine. People were convinced of the idea so much that their anxiety began to show visible signs of reduction. This is why medical trials usually have a test group along with a trial group: one group is given the real medicine while the other takes placebos. If the medicine has a much greater effect than the placebo group, then the medicine definitely works. If it has more or less the same results provided by the placebo group, then technically there is no point in manufacturing the medicine.

Imagine that, our minds are so powerful that they can even convince the body that unreal medicines are capable of having physical effects.

The above two examples show you the power of mental manipulations. You don't need to have the power of the X-Men or a futuristic ray gun to control people. Mental manipulation is simply the result of the mind being made to work against us through various psychological techniques.

Which is why it is important to understand our mind better.

It's time to step out of the light and venture forth into the dark side of the mind.

CHAPTER 1: THE DARK OF THE MIND: HEADING DEEPER INTO HUMAN CONSCIOUSNESS

Our perception of our mind is flawed.

We are bombarded with so much information, that what we know of the human mind is governed by what we see in the news, movies, or probably on social media. Let us look at some of the perceptions we have of our mind and the reality behind those assumptions.

We Have a Left Brain and a Right Brain

Complete myth. There have never been studies conducted to show that people are dominated by one side of the brain over the other. On the contrary, a study has been conducted to debunk the myth.

In 2013, researchers from the University of Utah examined the brains of more than 1,000 people in an attempt to discover if there were "left brained" or "right brained" people (Nielsen, Zielinski, Ferguson, Lainhart & Anderson, 2013). What they discovered was that there was no major difference in the left- or right-sided brain activities of people. The MRI scans showed that the neural networks all over the brain showed more or less the same levels of activities.

We Only Use 10% of Our Brain

If you have watched the movie Limitless or Lucy, then you might notice that ordinary people suddenly become smarter or stronger once they have unlocked the full potential of the human brain.

If only it were true.

Think of it this way. We, humans, have evolved to be the smartest creatures on the planet and that is not a statement made out of hubris, but out of factual information. It would be such a terrible situation to have spent so much energy and time evolving such a complex brain only to realize we can't even use 90% of it. What was the purpose of evolution then?

According to researcher Barry Gordon, who is also the neurologist at the Johns Hopkins School of Medicine in Baltimore, the myth of the brain using 10 percent of its capacity is almost "laughable" (Boyd, 2008). That's definitely going to put a big dent in the beliefs of many people.

Men and Women Learn Differently

There has never been a shred of scientific evidence to prove it. In fact, numerous studies have debunked the myth that women are better at multitasking than men, which arose because research showed that women's brains have slightly denser connections.

These myths show us our current perceptions of our brain. Chances are that even if you were already aware of the reality of most of all of the above myths, chances are that you know somebody who still believes that performing a few Sudoku exercises will unlock his or her hidden potential.

Science has not yet uncovered all the mysteries of the human mind. In fact, researchers are still pondering about how the brain creates consciousness. While consciousness is not unique to humans, as animals have neural activity that denotes the presence of some sort of consciousness. However, this is a theory that is debated often, because no one understands the extent and nature of consciousness in humans. How can we define properly something that is not tangible?

Because of this, no one can understand our psychology well. While many secrets have been explained with certain theories, there are still a number of mysteries that have no definite answers.

What is the relationship between the physical world and our subjective experience? How is it that humans are so quickly able to understand and interpret the external world? In fact, here is a question that many scientists are still trying to answer: why do we sleep?

All of these myths point out to one thing.

We do not fully understand the human mind.

This brings us to Dark Psychology.

Most people think that we are all born like an empty slate and that the experiences that we collect decide the personality that we adopt later in life. That is partly true. You see, our darker nature has had a longer time to stay with us. It has been there during our birth and even when we develop control mechanisms against it, we are doing it slowly, over the course of many years. This means that it has the upper hand when it comes to revealing itself.

Which brings us to our conscious. More specifically, our subconscious.

CLASH OF THE TITANS: CONSCIOUS VS SUBCONSCIOUS MIND

In the battle between your conscious and subconscious mind, which do you think would come out on top as the victor?

At this point, you are probably feeling confident about the fact that you are in control of your mind. Sure, there are times when you have a few mental "hiccups" but, for the most part, you feel like you are consciously putting in an effort to control your reaction to the events happening in your life.

That is a powerful thought to have. But that is all it is; a powerful thought. Remember the myths we talked about?

Well, get ready for one of the biggest ones there is.

Think about this scenario.

You are heading towards a particular destination that you are familiar with. It could be your home or to the local store, but it is a place you have gone to enough times that you know the route like the back of your hand. On the way there, you notice an advertisement for a soft drink. You immediately start thinking about your favorite soft drinks. Thoughts of soft drinks lead to ruminations about your childhood and the drinks you shared with your friends. This eventually makes you wonder where your friends are right now. That's right! Isn't that one friend somewhere in town? Maybe the two of you could hit the local bar. Wait a minute, wasn't there a special deal on Thursday nights where you get a drink free with-

Hold on.

You have just reached your destination.

But what just happened? You don't recollect most of the journey at all.

What you just experienced is a psychological phenomenon called highway hypnosis. In this phenomenon, you leave the driving to your subconscious brain while your conscious part focuses on the thoughts zipping through your mind. It's like going on autopilot, leaving the task of driving to your subconscious self.

In fact, think of your situation right now.

You are reading this book. But have you thought about who is regulating your breathing, body temperature, posture, whether your mouth if closed or hanging open, how many times you blink, and other functions?

It is quite odd to focus on these things, isn't it? We never really pay attention to them because doing so would distract us from the things that truly matter. Additionally, it causes a fair amount of stress as well. And that's not something we want to add onto a mental plate that is already full of thoughts about bills, deadlines at work, groceries, commitments, future goals, and anything else that is already pushing our mental capabilities to the limit.

We are confident that our conscious mind is so powerful that we fail to realize just how much power the subconscious mind is exerting.

Priming

Let us look at this study conducted by two researchers in 2006. Chen Bo-Zhong from the University of Toronto and Katie Liljenquist from Northwestern University prepared a study in which participants were asked to recall a terrible sin from their past. They were then asked to explain how the sin made them feel.

Once done, half of the people were allowed to wash their hands.

It was then that the two researchers asked the participants if they would be willing to help out a fellow student with a particular thesis, free of cost. Only 41 percent of those who had washed their hands agreed to help while more than 70% of the people who did not wash their hands agreed to help out the student.

Why?

According to the researchers, those who had washed their hands made a subconscious connection with the idea of "washing away their sins". In our culture, we use the idea of purity and cleanliness to describe both physical states and various situations. A corrupt politician is considered "dirty". A person with a lot of compassion is said to have a "pure soul". Even many of the major religions in the world utilize the act of washing in their rituals. Muslims use the act of Wudu, which is essentially washing parts of their body before conducting their prayers. The idea behind Wudu is that it "cleans" people and that state of cleanliness is how they should present themselves before God. Christians use the idea of washing in the ritual of baptism, where the person is immersed in water to "purify" them. In similar ways, Hinduism uses water to wash their idols and clean their houses to keep away "evil influences".

In a similar manner, half of the participants of the aforementioned study had felt that they had washed away their sins. And now that they were relatively free of their sins, they didn't have any lingering feelings of guilt or remorse. The other group, however, felt like they needed to make up for their sins with a good deed.

But how did these participants reach such a conclusion? Did they knowingly make such a decision? Not at all. The participants were not told that the student was part of the study.

So, how did they form such connecting thoughts?

Priming.

In short, they were primed to think in such a manner because the idea of "washing away their sins" was already embedded in their minds.

When certain stimuli from the past affect the way we behave and react in the present, then the process is called priming. Guess what part of your brain controls priming?

If you guessed the subconscious mind, then you are absolutely right. You are probably thinking: where exactly am I going with this?

All in good time. Because before I reveal the conclusion, we need to first explore our emotions a little.

Emotions

Do you consider yourself a logical person?

Do you believe that decisions are purely logical conclusions made after evaluating all the facts presented to people?

Well, you have another thing coming.

Antonio Damasio, a neuroscientist, made a remarkable discovery (Lenzen, 2005). He was studying people who had suffered damage to the part of their brains where emotions are created. The obvious conclusion was that while these people could function fairly normally, they were unable to feel emotions.

However, the unobvious discovery that he made was that these people found it difficult to make even the simplest of decisions. Queries such as what food to eat, which would not be a problem for us to answer, became complex riddles for the people involved in the study.

Damasio soon came to realize something; our emotions affect a large number of the decisions we make every day. Even though we think we are rational about our approach, there is an emotional cause underlying our decisions.

The conscious part of our brain is the rational side. The subconscious brain is our emotional side. We, as emotional creatures, are influenced immensely by our subconscious mind.

And this is where we understand something else.

Priming + Emotions = A Powerful Subconscious

In a study conducted by scientists from the Max Planck Institute for Human Cognitive and Brain Sciences in Leipzig along with researchers from Bernstein Center for Computational Neuroscience in Berlin (Max-Planck-Gesellschaft, 2008), a brain scanner was used to investigate just how the brain makes decisions. More importantly, they were focused on finding out about decisions that are made using our conscious mind.

What they discovered was rather surprising and might change our notions of how we actually use our brain. Based on their studies, our decision-making process is a subconscious activity to a surprising degree.

This point illustrates something important: Our subconscious mind is more powerful than we give it credit for.

Whenever we think that our conscious mind has made some connections, the subconscious mind is secretly influencing us without our knowledge. The entire act feels so clandestine and we are barely aware of it. But our subconscious mind is also emotional. It has collected our experiences and memories. It has collated our fears, likes, dislikes, and other feedback and created a repository of all the information that makes us what we are today. Using this repository, it gives us suggestions on what our decisions are supposed to be, fueled by emotions we never knew guided our thoughts.

The subconscious mind's ability to use emotions also affects the act of priming. When we receive primes, they are mostly emotional. Think of the study where people washed their hands and refused to help out a fellow student because they felt absolved of their sins. Any rational person would have paused, evaluated their thought process, and decided that if they had the time, they could help out the student indeed.

But our minds are not as rational as we thought.

In short, our subconscious mind affects a large part of our decisions, many of them through the process of priming. As our subconscious mind is mostly guided by emotions, a large part of the primes we receive are also emotions.

And our emotions are pretty dark.

THE DARK MIND RISES

Our darker side has had a longer time to influence us than our lighter side. We were born as impulsive creatures, giving our dark sides free rein on our psyche. This dark side also had much influence on our emotions.

And we know how powerful our emotions are, especially when guided by our subconscious.

Our darker emotions are more powerful and more evolved than our lighter ones. We are quick to anger. Even those who have managed to control their anger have only been able to do so because they had first admitted that anger is easy to display. They understood that their negative emotions are much more volatile and it is only after this acceptance that they were able to manage them.

Getting in touch with our dark side is easy. It is like having a library that has been set up since we were born. All we need to do is *react impulsively*.

That is why it becomes easier for people to victimize and manipulate others. They have so much anger, shame, or even envy that they are ready to retaliate. At the end of the day, that is what Dark Psychology is all about; focusing on those aspects of human behavior where people act upon their dark impulses.

And that is why you need to be prepared. For the most part, victims of mental manipulation are unaware that they are being manipulated. Think back to the events of Jonestown, a cult run by the infamous Jim Jones (Kennedy, 2018). Most of the people followed his rhetoric and preaching, unaware that their minds were being snared by a vicious predator. And on November 18, 1978, when Jim Jones gave the order for his followers to take their own lives, they did.

More than 900 people ended their lives based on the words of one person.

A New Hope

So what does this mean?

Is our subconscious way beyond help? Can we not do something to change the way our subconscious reacts to things? Are we forever doomed to succumb to the dark machinations of our mind, unable to change the outcome?

That's not true.

Have you ever seen people who start off their day by listening to a few motivational quotes? Or perhaps the colleague in the office who likes to decorate his or her workspace with plants? How about people who enjoy a nice cup of coffee in the morning?

You see, all of these actions are a way to prime ourselves. People use motivational quotes because they want to start their day with a little empowerment. That way, no matter what challenges they face, their mind automatically falls back on the quote they read from Albert Einstein, Henry Ford, or maybe even Barack Obama. Eventually, their mind becomes saturated with enough motivation that no matter how complex or intense the challenges are, it is ready with a responsive action.

In the same way, a lot of the techniques that are mentioned in this book are like priming your mind. You are preparing yourself by setting up strong defenses. At the same time, you are learning some techniques that will help you get the advantage in a situation.

But before we venture forth into learning about the various Dark Psychology secrets, we are going to understand some of the personality types that are classified as dark

CHAPTER 2: THE FOUR HORSEMEN: DARK PERSONALITY TRAITS

When you begin to analyze dark personality types, then you come across something known as the Dark Triad.

The concept of the Dark Triad was first discovered by a duo of researchers named Kevin Williams and Delroy Paulhus in 2002. The word "triad" in the name has no symbolic reference to the infamous mafia group Triad. Rather, it is in reference to the three personality types that make up the Dark Triad; Narcissism (which is a sense of entitled self-importance), Psychopathy (cynicism, callousness, and a total disregard for the rules of morality), and Machiavellianism (the ability to be deceitful and strategically exploit others). Even though the Dark Triad traits are mostly studied among criminals, the researchers believe that we, as human beings, possess at least some qualities of the three (our dark side is pretty experienced after all, as we had seen in the previous chapter).

When we are examining Dark Psychology, however, something happens. Despite there being three major traits in Dark Triad, the same cannot be said true of Dark Psychology.

In Dark Psychology, one cannot simply use the term Psychopathy to explain everything. Because while some people totally enjoy a sense of callousness, there are those who simply enjoy making victims helpless just because they take some twisted pleasure out of it.

That is why Dark Psychology is a mix of the Dark Triad and a fourth element.

And what is this fourth element?

For that, we are going to use the "dark personality" traits that were established by Del Paulhus, a Personality Psychologist at the University of British Columbia (Kennedy, 2018). According to him, there are four traits that comprise a dark personality. We have already seen three of them in the forms of Narcissism, Psychopathy, and Machiavellianism. The fourth trait (or element) is Sadism.

Let us examine these traits. More importantly, let us examine these traits with reference to the people who exhibit them. Let's start with Narcissism.

THE FIRST HORSEMAN: FAMINE | THE NARCISSIST

In Greek mythology, Narcissus was the son of the River God Cephisus and the nymph Liriope. His beauty was exemplary to an extent that even the God Apollo loved him for it and his spectacular physique.

But alas, his looks would eventually be his downfall.

One day, Narcissus was walking by a lake when he decided to stop for a drink. As he reached out to get some water, he saw his own reflection and found that he was entranced by it. As he gazed at this reflection, he realized that he could not obtain the object of his desire and died from his sorrow.

These days, the story is used to describe the folly of people who have an unhealthy obsession with themselves, where they have an excessive need for admiration and attention while also exhibiting a lack of empathy for others. Such people are labeled as *Narcissists* by the psychological community.

However, what the story fails to highlight is the dangers that Narcissists cause to others. It is true that Narcissism is a path that often leads to self-destruction, but it also a path wrought with the destruction of others.

When Narcissism Becomes Dark

We are all proud of ourselves to a certain degree. We cannot bear the idea of someone attacking our character or personality. It makes us defensive.

But Narcissists take this to a whole new level.

According to many therapists (Wedge, 2015), the feelings of superiority and grandiosity that Narcissists feel are a result of their fragile, and sometimes broken, self. Researchers believe that under all the gloating and heightened feelings of self-importance lies a defense mechanism. This defense holds back feelings of self-loathing, pain, and a fragmented ego.

Psychologists have narrowed down some of the traits of Narcissists and discovered that they:

- Exaggerate the talents that they possess or the achievements that they have accomplished. They do not mind embellishing facts to seem better than they actually are.

- Possess a hyperbolic sense of self-importance that often fails to recognize or overshadows the importance of others.

- Expect people to recognize them as superior, even though they have not necessarily achieved anything to warrant such a status.

- Become preoccupied with fantasies about beauty, power, success, and brilliance, often projecting them into a status or symbol of perfection.

- Believe in the idea that since they are superior, they have to be associated with similar people.

- Expect others to give them special favors and unquestionable compliance to their suggestions without expecting anything in return.

- Falsely believe that any criticism that they receive is purely because others are envious of them.

- Insist that they only deserve the best, even if they have not put in the effort to achieve what they seek.

- Feel comfortable taking advantage of others to get what they want and, in some cases, believing that the role of others is to help them get what they want.

With these traits, Narcissists are capable of doing a little or considerable harm to others, which can be either emotional, physical, or psychological. But here's something most people do not know about Narcissism. Sometimes, it may not be obvious.

The field of psychology has discovered two kinds of Narcissists, Overt and Covert.

As the name such suggests, Overt Narcissists have traits that can be easily noticed by others. On the other hand, Covert Narcissists are not easy to spot. They are often introverted and display their traits easily in front of someone that they trust. However, the term covert does not mean that some people are sneaky or use deceptive tactics. It simply means that Covert Narcissists do not come out as Narcissists, unlike their Overt counterparts.

Regardless of what form of Narcissism one has, he or she eventually falls into two camps.

In one camp, people are willing to change. They understand that they have faults within themselves and that they would like to change their behavior and personality.

Then there are people who belong to the other camp. These Narcissists are capable of inflicting great psychological and physical pain on others and remained unmoved by the anguish that others feel. They can be cold and calculated. They employ their manipulative tendencies to their full capacity. To them, almost any line can be crossed to achieve what they want. Additionally, they can change their personalities in a flash. They might appear so charming that you might not even stop to think that they are Narcissists.

Here is a scenario that can explain what happens to people who become victims of people with Narcissism.

Narcissists who can be charming hang on to every word that the other person says. They can seem genuinely interested to a point that they make people feel like they are the center of attention. They are capable of making eye contact comfortably, giving the impression that they are confident. They can easily compliment people of things that they find important, such as the way they think, their appearance, their clothes, and so on. In fact, such Narcissists can make people feel genuinely valued, heard, and cherished.

Eventually, their victims become comfortable around them. They feel that they have found a good friend, partner, or acquaintance.

People who end up in relationships with Narcissists, who can be manipulative, have one of the most difficult times navigating the relationship. They start noticing the little oddities in the beginning.

The Narcissist might slowly start losing interest in his/her partner. The partner, on the other hand, is left wondering if it was something that they did. The frequency of being interrupted increases, making the partners feel like their voice isn't heard. Eventually, the situation intensifies. The Narcissist begin to openly criticize their partners and begin to place themselves as the center of the conversation. Other people seem to interest them more, leaving their partners baffled and left out.

This turns into a very serious situation: an abusive relationship.

In an abusive relationship, the person being abused can suffer in a myriad of ways. The abuses do not have to strictly be physical. Victims can suffer because of psychological and emotional attacks as well.

This is what happens in a relationship with certain Narcissists. The victim begins to feel bombarded by psychological attacks. In many cases, the victims remain silent because they had originally perceived the abuser as someone who is charming and wonderful. The victims imagine that the relationship has turned around because of something that they did. In other words, victims feel like they are the perpetrators of the damage caused to the relationship, not knowing the psychological trap that they have placed themselves in.

Before you know it, the Narcissists have complete control over their victims.

The above scenario is just one way that Narcissists can use mental manipulation to their advantage.

But while some Narcissists are capable of using their behavior and charisma for a lot of harm, know that every Narcissist that you come across is a Villain. Some have genuine problems that they would like to take care of. Others have character flaws that require a bit of attention and understanding.

We are not focused on people who have faults. We know that everyone in the world does. Remember that every single person in the world has some degree of each of the Dark Triad. We are not all perfect.

However, we are focusing on those Narcissists who take pleasure in using Dark Psychology techniques to manipulate others or cause psychological harm to them.

THE SECOND HORSEMAN: CONQUEST | THE MACHIAVELLIAN

Niccolò Machiavelli was a Florentine philosopher in the 16 century who would go on to create some of the most influential works in philosophical history.

According to him, any virtue - including honesty - can be sacrificed if other, more nefarious tactics, such as force, deception, and treachery can accomplish a particular job faster. In other words, he wanted people in positions of power to forego all notions of nobility and adopt a Machiavellianism form of leadership. I don't think Niccolò was invited to a lot of parties.

In psychology, Machiavellianism takes on a more sinister meaning.

You see, the term refers to anyone is does not *choose* to be manipulative. Rather, he or she *is* manipulative (Hartley, 2015). In other words, Machiavellians are people who simply have a natural tendency to consider others as a steppingstone to get what they want.

We have seen the various traits of Narcissists in the previous section. In a similar way, let us see what psychologists have to say about Machiavellianism. According to them, Machiavellians:

- Tend to focus solely on their interests, goals, and ambitions. Everyone else's concerns are merely interruptions or distractions.

- Give priority to power and money over relationships. They can easily discard relationships to attain more power and wealth.

- Appear confident and charming, but are, in reality, already marking the weaknesses of the other person and the opportunities they can use.

- Comfortable manipulating and exploiting others to get ahead in life without feeling even the slightest remorse.

- Are capable of easily lying and deceiving others when required.

- Enjoy using flattery often without having any honest intentions.

- Lack any form of values or principles to guide their actions.

- Often come across as hard-to-get, difficult to understand, or aloof when some of those actions are used to garner attention.

- View morality and goodness through a cynical lens, often posturing that such values are not required in society.

- Are comfortable causing physical harm to others to achieve their goals. Sometimes, they might cause harm directly, especially if they would like to absolve themselves of the act. But they are capable of watching harm come to another person and not lend a hand to help.

- Possess a low degree of empathy. In some cases, empathy is so low that it almost seems non-existent.

- Avoid emotional attachments or commitments. Even when they do, it is to achieve a specific goal, after which they disentangle themselves from their attachments.

- Do not easily reveal their true intentions. They are also constantly wearing a mask to disguise their true nature.

- Are more likely to engage in casual sex encounters.

- Can read people easily and understand social situations.

- Can appear completely engrossed in a social situation but, in reality, lack the warmth required for such interactions.

- Might sometimes not be aware of the consequences of their actions.

- Are sometimes not capable of understanding their own emotions.

In The Shadows

If you think about it, most people are aware of Narcissists, Psychopaths, and even Sadists. However, Machiavellians seem to go under the radar of observation. Why is this so? Is it because they prefer it that way?

According to psychologist Jeremy Dean (Dean, 2018), that might just be the case.

You see, Machiavellians are concerned about their reputation (we noticed how much they value power and money). They understand that if their reputation were to be affected, then they might suffer the consequences of it. And to them, failure is not an option.

In the world on Dark Psychology, what makes Machiavellians dangerous is not just their ability to cold-heartedly manipulate people, but their ability to be rather intelligent.

In fact, ever heard of the term fluid intelligence?

Raymond B. Cattell was the first to suggest there being the existence of two forms of intelligence, fluid and crystallized (Vinney, 2019). The idea is rather simple. People who have fluid intelligence are able to use their logic to solve problems easily in novel or new situations in creative ways. On the other hand, crystallized intelligence relies on using past knowledge and experiences.

Recent studies have shown that fluid intelligence is linked to Machiavellianism (Dolan, 2018). In fact, these studies are also focused on finding out the "evil genius" aspect of Machiavellianism. This aspect focuses on the idea that Machiavellians tend to have higher intelligence than regular people because of their ability to strategize and manipulate in various situations.

So imagine this scenario: someone who is so adept at manipulating people and does not feel a single trace of guilt or remorse about the act, just so happens to also have the ability to use his or her intelligence to adapt to any situation.

That is a dangerous combination of skills right there.

THE THIRD HORSEMAN: DEATH | THE PSYCHOPATH

Charles Manson. Ted Bundy. Jack the Ripper. Aileen Wuornos.

If you recognize these names, then you know what you are looking at is a list of famous Psychopaths.

If you look at the lineup of Netflix shows in the year 2018, then you might notice a jump in the number of shows that focus on Psychopaths. Hollywood has also been fascinated with Psychopaths, creating some notable fictional characters like Norman Bates, Alex Forrest, and Patrick Bateman. But why is there such an interest in Psychopaths? What makes these people the focus of attention repeatedly?

Part of it has to do with the fact that many are trying to understand just why someone would commit extreme violence without a shred of remorse. How can someone cause so much harm without even exhibiting the slightest bit of empathy?

Psychopathy is one of the more difficult disorders to diagnose or even spot. This probably has to do with the fact that a Psychopath can appear completely normal, even charming, intelligent, and eloquent. However, underneath all that facade is a person capable of violence and rage, and who is devoid of conscience and empathy.

Take, for example, the case of Jeffrey Dahmer. This notorious serial killer took the lives of 17 men between 1978 and 1991 (Biography.com Editors, 2014). He was discovered to have strangled the victims and kept souvenirs of them in his refrigerator. When authorities entered his home, it was also revealed that he had engaged in acts of cannibalism.

But what captivated people about his story was not the brutality of his acts. Rather, it was the simple fact that on the surface, he was a polite, charming, and unassuming man. Nothing about him could indicate that he was a Psychopath.

Typically, Psychopathy is associated with unusual emotional responses and certain antisocial behaviors. However, one of the common traits in Psychopathy - as we had seen earlier - is lowered empathic responses. A Psychopath is also known to respond poorly to society's standards of mortality. This means that he or she has complete disregard to how people should treat each other in society. However, this should not be confused with those who exhibit behavior of rebelliousness. Someone who scorns society's established rules does not automatically become a Psychopath.

According to psychologists, Psychopaths:

- Exhibit a complete lack of empathy, remorse, or conscience.

- Do not exhibit the right feelings or emotions based on the situation.

- Are impulsive and typically have weak control over their impulses. They cannot easily divert their need for gratification. Additionally, they have limited control over their behavior.

- Can appear charming, but the entire act is superficial.

- Do not accept responsibility for their actions and are usually irresponsible.

- Have an inflated sense of their own worth.

- Are extremely selfish. They are concerned about what they would like to do without any focus on the consequences of their actions.

- Can identify between what's right and wrong, but does not allow himself or herself to be governed by such rules.

- Are pathological liars and do not have trouble coming up with a lie as the situation demands it.

- Are extremely cunning and can be manipulative as well.

- Display signs of a parasitic lifestyle, which is a selfish and exploitative dependency on others. Psychopaths enjoy taking advantage of others to help them live their lives.

- Have a strong craving for some sort of stimulation. It does not have to be sexual stimulation, but they cannot control the urge to do something to make their life exciting. This is different from a person who simply chooses to have a sense of adventure or novel experience in his or her life. In the case of Psychopaths, they are definitely thinking of causing harm to someone to create that stimulation.

When Psychopathy Evolves

According to psychologists, adult Psychopathy is mostly impervious to treatments. This is because no pill can bring back feelings of empathy. No treatment can prevent someone from harming someone else in a cold and calculated manner.

When Psychopaths enter society, they present themselves in a favorable manner to others. In fact, many can even function normally in society. However, most of the characteristics and attributes that Psychopaths hold on to are considered predatory, as they hone their skills to target their "prey".

Once they have narrowed down their victim, the inability to form empathy or genuine bond with the person allows them to have a heightened sense of clarity regarding their prey's behavior. This allows them to plan their actions, often fantasizing about what they would do to their victims.

When it comes to Dark Psychology, Psychopaths cannot be easily distinguished from the crowd. But with the right tools, people can protect themselves from the influence of one.

THE FOURTH HORSEMAN: WAR | THE SADIST

One of the things that the movie Fifty Shades of Grey revealed was (apart from a horrendous plot and terrible acting) the nature of Sadism. In particular, the movie projected the very graphic nature of Sadism. One might think that only certain people (such as the titular character of Mr. Grey in the movie) are capable of Sadism. There are truly some unique people in the world aren't there?

However, every person on the planet exhibits some level of Sadism.

Sadism was once attributed to the Dark Triad. Personality psychologists began to understand that Sadism might require its own special spot, mostly for the fact that it is a complex subject to tackle. The main reason for this complexity is the various degrees in which it can take place. Which eventually brings us back to the earlier point made about how every individual in the world has a degree of Sadism.

You could enjoy blowing characters in a video game to tiny bits. The sports game that you watch gets even more exciting when players engage in a clash with the opponents. We even view movies that have more "intense" sequences, showcasing our urge to see more suffering develop for the characters before they triumph, else the movie is boring. Each of us take pleasure in everyday experiences where cruelty is displayed to a certain degree.

Think about it this way. When someone offends us and later ends up physically hurting themselves, we feel a sense of satisfaction at their pain. We, of course, chalk it up to Karma, telling ourselves that the person deserved it. The fact that the person deserves it or not is irrelevant. The idea that we found the entire experience satisfying is what is important.

For most people, while they do harbor a small degree of Sadism, they do not indulge in it to great lengths. They don't always encourage the behavior in themselves or seek to work on it. Most of the time, such Sadistic behaviors are fairly impulsive. They last for a brief moment and disappear. Additionally, people do not inflict harm using their Sadistic urges.

According to psychologists, Sadists:

- Have a ruthless and cruel behavior The take a twisted sense of pleasure from inflicting pain on others, especially those who they deem inferior or weaker.

- Do not discriminate between humans and animals in that they do not care if they have to inflict pain on any creature. They also find the pain suffered by others amusing.

- Are capable of lying and deceiving others blatantly, even their loved ones or people they consider close.

- Love to impose their dominance on people. With such dominance also comes restrictions; Sadists force other people to confine their actions, behavior, and lives to a set of agreeable rules or patterns.

- Enjoy controlling people to a great degree, even going so far as to humiliate them to get what they want.

- Are also classified as Sexual Sadists, referring to people who enjoy ruthless and painful sexual acts and derive pleasure by inflicting torture on their partners.

- Believe that they should be in power. They may enter into a deep rage if things do not go their way.

- Need to validate their position constantly. They may go out of their way to spontaneously bring others down for the purpose.

- They are known to disregard the authority of others, as they feel they should be in positions of authority.

- Are fascinated by weapons, physical combat (such as martial arts), and torture techniques that they can use against another person.

- Can remodel their social functioning to fit the situation, not only because they can arrive as the most interesting and most knowledgeable person in the group, but also so that they can work their manipulative abilities on their next victim.

The Aggression of Sadism

In a series of studies conducted by psychologist David Chester and his colleagues (Chester & DeWall, 2017), participants were asked to go through certain experiments to gauge the connection between Sadism and pleasure. In one such experiment, the participants were asked to imagine that a voodoo doll was their worst enemy. They were then given pins that they could use to puncture the doll. At the end of the experiment, the participants were asked if they thought the real person might have felt some harm from their actions. The participants responded by claiming that their actions did, in fact, inflict pain on real people.

The voodoo dolls did nothing. They were just that: dolls. But the participants were convinced that by stabbing the dolls with pins, they were, in a small way, causing pain to the person the dolls represented. This idea gave them satisfaction because to think otherwise would mean a sense of disappointment, which the participants could not accept.

Sadists could also belong to a group called Sexual Sadism, which involves feelings of sexual pleasure or excitement as a result of pain, humiliation, or suffering inflicted on others. This pain, humiliation, or suffering may be physical or psychological. But the end result is the same; it evokes sexual satisfaction in the perpetrator.

Consider the case of Ariel Castro.

After kidnapping three women and imprisoning them in his house for years, he subjected them to numerous humiliations and sexual abuse. The women were, of course, rescued eventually and Castro was served with life imprisonment.

Psychologists evaluating his case discovered that he had a Sadistic personality disorder. In fact, he showed no remorse after he was imprisoned, accepting what he did with a sense of cold apathy.

In Dark Psychology, Sadists are methodical. They do not immediately reveal their true intentions. They are calculating and often appear normal. In fact, in the case of Ariel Castro, he would go on to live a normal life while keeping the three women chained in his basement. For all those who knew him, he was a normal member of the community.

Drawing the Line

They say that knowledge is power.

That is true in almost every case. When we have the right knowledge, we become more aware. Take for example all that you have learned about the dark personality traits in this chapter. Using the information provided to you, you can be more analytically about people and understand motivations more clearly.

But with that knowledge, comes a sense of responsibility as well.

You might think that many of the researchers who engage in the findings of dark traits have some sort of dark personality within them. After all, how else can they understand these people in such an intimate way? The reality is quite far from the truth.

Psychologists try to understand the human mind, not so we can start scrutinizing people closely, but so that we understand that there are many components that make up the mind of a person. These components, in turn, create the personality, responses, and behavior of the person.

In other words, not everything is as simple as black and white.

Psychology aims to shed light on human behavior so that you do not get swayed by popular opinions, whether you see them online, on TV, or in your favorite movies. That creepy kid on TV who turns out to be a psychotic killer might resemble someone you know, but that does not mean they share the same traits or are capable of the same acts.

And this sense of awareness is important to understand.

You see, it is easy to look at all the dark personalities mentioned above and start making connections in real life. Is that colleague of yours, who pretends to be charming, secretly hiding bodies in his or her refrigerator? Is that friend you met at the supermarket - who is known to lie consistently - a Sadist in secret?

Hardly. Remember that we all share dark personality traits. We all have a bit of Narcissism, Psychopathy, Sadism, and Machiavellianism in us. But those traits are not born to cause harm to others. Rather, they are constructs that we use to help us navigate the complexities, tragedies, emotions, and challenges of life. For example, when we go through a tragedy - say the loss of a loved one - we often become consistent liars, telling everyone around us that we are fine when we are not. We become withdrawn, choosing to remain in our own company. Even when we are in social occasions, we pretend to display signs of affection and normal social behavior. In many cases, because of the surge of emotions running through us, we automatically lash out at people.

But does that make us Psychopaths?

Let us take another example. Let us assume that you notice that one of your friends exhibits superficial charm. He or she is capable of complimenting people, but you know that those compliments are hollow and not genuine. Your friend also likes to constantly be the center of attention.

Now in such a scenario, your friend does have traces of Narcissism. But you cannot automatically relegate him or her to the dark personality section.

Maybe your friend has a genuine problem with low self-esteem. Perhaps he or she is trying to engage with other people, slowly building up the confidence to have genuine conversations. Your friend might have suffered a past tragedy, preventing him or her from having meaningful relationships, which eventually drained their levels of confidence. Sure, your friend is trying to be the center of attention, but that is probably because he or she has been neglected many times in their lives, often by people close to them.

In such scenarios, you should not be judging them. Rather, you should be out there helping them. Bipolar disorder, anxiety, anger management, and post-traumatic stress disorder are all genuine psychological issues that people suffer from. With such people, the necessary step to take is to reach out to them and give them help and support.

This is why, when dealing with dark personalities, there is usually a list of traits that decide whether a person is Narcissistic to a point where they have entered the dark side. It is for this reason that psychology never mentions a couple or few points to indicate whether someone has a certain type of mental disorder, psychological problem, or dark personality. This could lead to a wrong diagnosis and misjudgments.

I have also included an exhaustive list of traits that psychologists themselves have used to determine dark personality types.

When you have identified a dark personality, however, you can move on to recognizing some of their tricks and preparing yourself for any eventual attacks.

CHAPTER 3: COVERT EMOTIONAL MANIPULATION

One of the traits that all four dark personality types share is their ability to covertly manipulate someone.

There is a reason why Covert Emotional Manipulation, or CEM for short, is being talked about first. This is because most mental manipulations and Dark Psychology tactics rely extensively or slightly on CEM. As you begin to delve deeper into the world of Dark Psychology, you might notice signs of CEM sprinkled throughout. In many ways, CEM is almost like a foundation for the many other characteristics and tactics in Dark Psychology.

Covert Emotional Manipulation is a method used by one person to influence the thoughts, behaviors, and feelings of another person in such a way that it cannot be detected by the person being manipulated.

One of the best ways to understand the concept is to break down each of the three words and examine them individually. That way, we receive a clearer picture of the technique.

Part 1: Covert

When a Manipulator is Covert, then he or she is able to hide some or all of their intentions. Some people may not have a lot of experience hiding emotions and it shows in their body language.

For example, the Manipulator might be smiling at you, but there is not honesty behind the expression. One of the ways to tell this is by looking at their eyes. When we are genuinely happy, our lower eyelids show wrinkles or indications of being stressed. You might also see a certain wrinkling pattern called "crow's feet" (by the way that it resembles the feet of the bird), at the corners of the eyes.

On the other hand, people who are adept at controlling their emotions might genuinely show that they are interested in you.

Victims of CEM usually do not recognize the manipulation in play. They believe that they are responding to the situation in a manner that is consistent with normality.

Part 2: Emotional

The "Emotional" part of CEM reveals the area of focus on the Manipulator. People who manipulate others use various tactics that target an individual's willpower, beliefs, principles, or even behavior. In CEM, the Manipulator is specifically focusing on the emotions of the victim and through the emotional states, affect the reality as well.

For example, if a person is in grief, then they are in a vulnerable state. They do not have full control over their emotions. Manipulators take advantage of this situation by inviting the grieving person — who is now their victim — into the Manipulator's personal space, such as their home or office. By such a simple action, Manipulators have pulled the victims into their territory. This makes the victims feel like a "guest" and they usually don't speak up, for fear of sounding rude or ungrateful. But this is also a way they become susceptible to the Manipulator's machinations. By targeting their emotions and bring them into a space that is not entirely comfortable to them, Manipulators target their emotions and eventually, change their reality. For the victim, the reality is that they feel even more vulnerable than before. They just don't know it yet.

Part 3: Manipulation

Lastly, we have the very act of Manipulation.

Many people are of the opinion that "influence" and "manipulation" are interchangeable terms. But there is a big difference between the two.

Let us try and use an example to highlight this. On June 27, 2013, two men dressed as missionaries knocked on a residence in Las Vegas (Bentz & Karimi,

2013). The owner of the residence, Terence Delucia, was apprehensive at first. But as the two men continued to chat to him about religion, he dropped his guard.

That was all the opportunity the men needed. The duo took out their guns, forced their way into his house and robbed him. During that time, his family was hidden in closets spread throughout the house.

Many people would say that the thieves influenced Delucia to drop his guard. But that is not true. There is a subtle difference.

Influence and manipulation seem related because they both contain elements of deception, dishonesty, and even subterfuge. The difference lies in the intent. People who influence others respect their well-being and lives. Those who use manipulation disregard any concern for the life, health, well-being, or safety of their victim.

Now let's go back to the example mentioned earlier. The two thieves were not influencing, they were manipulating. They definitely intended to cause harm to the people in the house. They were not about to show remorse to anyone.

Perhaps the best way to sum up the difference between an Influencer and a Manipulator is through the statements below:

Influencer - "I want you to listen to me because I know what's good for you or what the right course of action is."

Manipulator - "I want you to listen to me because I am going to control you to get what I want."

THE SPHERES OF MANIPULATION

Broadly speaking, there are four main areas, or spheres, where convert manipulation can be placed. These are the spheres of manipulation and they are personal, professional, romantic, and family. Among the four spheres mentioned the romantic sphere of life is perhaps the one that includes the most cases of CEM and also allows the Manipulator to be the deadliest. This is because, in a romantic relationship, the Manipulator slowly works to gain the trust of the person, alienate him or her from friends and family, and even gain a sense of devotion from the victim.

Once you are able to understand the concept of CEM and how they apply in each of the four spheres, you will be able to create defenses against it. You will be able to recognize it no matter what situation you find yourself in.

We have already seen some of the common spheres of manipulation. But just like there are common spheres, there are also certain traits that govern the Manipulator in those spheres.

Let us try and examine them.

Personal Sphere

When it comes to your personal space, then it usually involves someone whom you consider a friend. Usually, we do not react well to the manipulations of strangers and casual acquaintances since we do not trust them entirely. However, I shall add a separate section to deal with manipulations from strangers.

So let us look at how you can defend against the so-called "friends". After all, if you are getting manipulated by someone you consider a friend, then you need to let them go.

One of the common ways a friend might manipulate you is by using your feelings of guilt, responsibility, sympathy, and obligation towards them. Here are some of the ways that they do it:

- You might find out that they tend to avoid confrontations. They do not directly speak to you if there is a problem. In fact, you might notice that they tend to use an intermediary to get the job done. For example, let us assume that you and your friend have a common friend named Susan, then you might find that Susan approaches you to tell you that your friend is upset about something that you have done.

- They do not listen to you often. You might find out that they are constantly engaged in their own activities. When conversations begin to turn towards you or a subject you want to focus on, the friend swivels it back around to them or their focus.

- You might find that they enjoy having most of the power. They prefer to have the last word in a conversation or ensure that they are always in control of a situation. You might find out that they often force you out of your comfort zone rather than help you get out of it. They do this so that you feel vulnerable and become dependent on them for guidance. This is another way in which they try to build on the power they have over you.

- They also tend to ask you a lot of favors. Typically, this is a form of a test, where the Manipulator is trying to see how far you are willing to go for them. With each new request that is fulfilled, the more emboldened the friend becomes in making the requests more challenging.

Now that you find yourself in a situation where your friend is clearly using you, there are a few things that you can do to try and resolve the situation with your friend.

- Do not engage in a meaningless charade. Do not mince words in front of them, else they think of it as weakness and not take you seriously. Ask them directly what they want. If your friend truly values the relationship, he or she will be honest with you. If you find out that your friend has responded honestly, then you know that your friendship can be repaired. If your friend is scheming, then they will usually try to over-rationalize things in order to exert control.

- Do not engage in complex mind games where you are answering vague, indirect, or unrelated questions or engage in pointless conversations. The more the situation plays out, the more opportunities your friend will have to manipulate you.

- Do not respond in anger. Your friend might try to rile you up because they want you to lose your calm and fail to form proper responses. Should you feel that you are not in the right frame of mind to handle a confrontation with your friend, then try and cool off first before dealing with your friend. Additionally, when you are able to maintain your composure, you do not give control of the situation over to your friend.

- Learn to say no. You have to start setting your boundaries. Remember that you are not being self-centered by saying no. Rather, you are establishing a relationship based on mutual respect and all good friendships have that level of respect. You do not have to justify why you are saying no. A simple, "I'm sorry but I cannot do that" will suffice. Refuse to provide justifications even when your friend insists.

- When your friend needs help, use your best judgment to decide whether you would like to help them or not. For example, if they ask you to come over and help them with a project that they are involved in but you are already busy with something, then you do not have to immediately agree to help them. You are free to say no.

- Friends who are manipulative like to make use of any advantage that they can get. Typically, they love to prey on your low self-esteem. If you find that your friend is trying to take a jab at your appearance, your life choices, your likes, or even your behavior, make a stand for yourself. For example, if your friend criticizes your fashion sense, simply remark that it makes you feel good. When you let your friend get a free pass, it only becomes worse.

- Do not let your friends constantly try to barge in on your personal affairs. Be confident about keeping some things to yourself, you do not always have to share everything with your friend.

Professional Sphere

Things become complicated when you are facing someone manipulative in your professional sphere. You would like to confront the person, but often find yourself worried about your job.

You simply have to browse the internet and you will find countless stories about people who have worked for a manager or with a colleague who is manipulative. These managers and colleagues can easily trigger feelings of fear, guilt, or remorse in a person.

Let us find out some of the ways that your boss or colleagues can get manipulative.

- You might find yourself in a situation where your boss or your colleague might find it necessary to remind you of the time they helped you out. In the case of your boss, he or she might also like to point out how difficult it is for people to make it in real life without the right opportunities, thereby referring that they are responsible for changing your life.

- Sometimes, the boss or colleague might choose to listen to you only when it suits them. This behavior is more noticeable in your boss. If they are intentionally neglecting you or playing dumb, then they are hoping that you suck up to them to receive further attention.

- Keeping you busy is good. But you might often find bosses who like to add too much to your plate to the point that it becomes overbearing. Certain bosses do this intentionally and they like to combine it with guilt-tripping over not completing your job. What they are trying to do is manipulate the situation towards their own benefit.

- If your colleague or boss refuses to face problems and tries giving excuses to avoid dealing with them, then that is a red flag. Manipulative people at the workforce distract you from what really matters, dodge issues presented to them, and prevent you from achieving your goals easily. They want you to feel tense and vulnerable.

- In many cases, your colleague or boss might use underhanded approaches to resolve a situation. For example, he or she might resort to scapegoating or blame-shifting. All of these are tactics to undermine your position or make you feel powerless.

- Someone who is manipulative at the workplace would like to ensnare you into their net of deception as quickly as possible. They do this by first making you trust them and eventually, drop your defenses. Once your defenses are down, they would like to find out about your personal life or your past. This information gives them ammunition that they can use against you in the future. If you find yourself receiving heaps of praise or becoming the boss's favorite as a new employee, then you better start questioning the motivations of the person.

- If your boss or colleague intentionally tries to make you feel dumb, then you are a victim of bullying. This act is another way to manipulate you by first making you feel inferior. When you feel defenseless and intimated, that's when they begin to work on the manipulation. Remember, there is a difference between intellectual stimulation and bullying. In one scenario, you are motivated to do better because the person is willing to teach and guide you. In the other, you feel humiliated or small by a person who employs knowledge to prove their superiority.

Once you understand what drives a manipulative boss, you can always take measures to deal with them.

- The first thing that you have to do is make sure that you are doing your job right and on time. This will automatically give you a sense of self-assurance. With this, you can face your boss and insist on keeping things professional.

- Do not let your emotions get the better of you. If you are entering a new job, be prepared to deal with everything in a rational manner. If you have been employed for a while, then it is time to practice controlling your emotions. Whenever you deal with your boss or colleague, use reason rather than emotions. Once you set down firm boundaries, people will find it difficult to introduce inappropriate or unacceptable habits in your relationship.

- Never wait for a situation to spiral out of control. Speak to someone else from management about the way you are treated by your boss or colleague. The more you speak to someone, the more they become aware of it.

- If your boss is dumping unwanted responsibilities on you, make sure that you point it out to them. This works particularly well if you have excellent performance in the responsibilities that you are already managing.

- If your boss has been avoiding talking to you about work-related issues or problems, be bold and ask him or her for a time that they would be comfortable talking about such issues. When they let you know a time, send them a reminder of a meeting scheduled at the time they are comfortable with. Bonus points for looping in your HR department as well!

- Whatever meeting you have with your boss should be in a written form. Recap the entire meeting in an email and send it across to your boss. That way, if he or she feels that something needs to be added or changed in the document, then they will let you know. In turn, you can check if what they have recommended makes sense to you. Once again, bonus points for looping in your HR team. Additionally, if you feel that your boss is ignoring a meeting or a crisis, follow it up with an email or text (something that can show that you have done your job). That way, you can explain your actions easily.

- Make sure you set limits to how your boss can talk to you or treat you in front of everyone. Let him or her know directly that should they need anything from you, they can call you to their office. If they have mistreated you in front of people, then inform them immediately.

- Do not mix business and personal life. No matter how friendly your boss may seem, he or she is still your boss. Keep your personal life away from your boss and ensure that every time you deal with him or her, you are doing it on a professional tone.

- If your boss or colleague is trying to use their intellect to make you seem ignorant, then make sure you bring the conversation to the topic at hand. Ask for direct responses. Do not indulge in their indirect form of conversation. If your boss or colleague side steps during a conversation or interaction, make sure you bring back their attention to what's important.

- Your confidence is your key. Do not lose it easily. When you have confidence, you restrain the person's efforts to manipulate you because they realize that they cannot place the intended effect on you.

Romantic Sphere

When love is in the air, we tend to forget a lot of warning signs about manipulation. We ignore our partner's habits and mental games. We do not take action to remedy the manipulation taking place because:

- We are probably thinking that perhaps we have done something wrong.

- We might be of the opinion that real relationships always have tests and that once those tests are passed, we create a strong relationship.

- We feel that our partner is probably going through a tough phase in his or her life.

- We are bound by certain obligations.

But none of the above reasons excuse the harm that you are experiencing because of the manipulations your partner is slowly placing on your mind. So what can you do in such circumstances?

Before we try and figure out the solution, we need to understand some of the ways manipulation can occur in a relationship.

- Typically, the way a partner tries to manipulate you is by establishing guilt. If your partner can make you feel guilty about something you have done (even though you have committed no mistakes), then your partner knows that you are willing to do whatever he or she says in the future. You might not even notice that your partner is making you feel guilty. Let's say you both go out for a movie and at the end of it, your partner says, "Well, I guess the movie was alright. It wasn't that great or anything. I mean, we could have gone to that other thing that I had suggested but I guess as long as you are happy, it is all that matters. I love you and to me, your happiness is my priority."

- Your partner might force their insecurities on you. If you have heard a statement that goes along the lines of "I had a terrible relationship in the past. My ex-partner cheated on me. That's why I don't want you to be with other men/women," then know that your partner is trying to manipulate you. This often happens when you are talking about his or her flaws. Your partner is simply trying to bring you back into his or her viewpoint.

- Often, your partner makes you responsible for his or her emotions. A common trick is to give you the power to form independent thoughts about their behavior. This is where you are free to form conclusions about their emotions. What is happening to them? Is there a way to change their current situation? But soon enough, they turn this scenario against you. They accuse you of not truly paying attention to them and then jumping to conclusions.

- You might notice that your partner is the one getting what he or she wants while your needs are not met. Eventually, your partner might explain to you that their needs are beneficial for both of you. While it is understandable to come to a compromise in a relationship, it is also important to see how much one person is compromising. If you are the one doing most of the compromising, then you might have to realize that it is not a compromise anymore.

- Your partner might sometimes use your good nature. Let's say that you both come across a puppy in the street. The non-manipulative method of talking about the situation would be to discuss with you what would happen if you get that puppy and come to a conclusion. Sure, you may not like the decision, but your partner shares the sadness you feel. The manipulative method would be to tell you that the puppy might die if you leave it out there. They might ask how you could be so callous and cold-hearted. This might seem like a trivial thing, but if you react to the situation, then the intensity of the manipulations gets worse. Your partner knows that you have a soft-spot and if you do not put your foot down, you are going to be taken for a ride.

As we have seen the many ways you can be manipulated, let us look at the steps you can take to defend yourself.

- Make sure that you put your foot down when you have to. When something seems unreasonable, uncomfortable, or unnecessary to you, talk to your partner about it and come to a mutual agreement. If your partner is incapable of compromises, then you need to let them know that you are not going to make giving up your needs a habit.

- Do not let your partner make you feel that making the best — and sometimes rational — choice is the wrong one. If your partner continues to pray on your sentiments, then it is time to have a rational conversation. Which brings us to the next point.

- Make sure you do not let your emotions get the better of you when your partner gets manipulative. When you show emotions, then your partner knows exactly how to trigger a response from you. Every time you would like to have a proper conversation with your partner, he or she will use your trigger points to change your focus.

- If you ever hear the phrase, "If you love me, then you should do (insert a request)." Do not encourage such train of thoughts from your partner. Instead, you can respond by saying, "I can still do that without having to stake my love on it."

- If you find yourself apologizing constantly, even when it was your partner's fault, then you have already been emotionally manipulated by him or her. When something is not your fault, take a deep breath. Evaluate the situation and think of what you can say other than an apology. How would you explain what really happened to your partner?

- Some people adopt a technique called gaslighting. In this process, your partner deliberately plays certain shady mind games. He or she pretends that you did not say certain things or that they did not say something, omits information, reinvents the truth, twists your words against you, or makes you feel like you forget things. You will eventually start believing that you are losing your mind. If your partner is using gaslighting techniques, then you need to get out of the relationship. It is pure emotional abuse and there is probably nothing you can do to stop it.

Family Sphere

Family is important. There is no doubt about that.

Parents, siblings, and close relatives are all capable of becoming abusive one way or the other. We don't usually notice signs of manipulation because we would never expect it to come from someone related to us by blood. In fact, manipulation from family members is probably the worst because you probably might not do anything about it because of your deep love for your family.

But being aware of such manipulations helps you lead a fulfilling life and even forge better bonds with family members.

Let us see some of the ways that your family can manipulate you.

- When it comes to your family, you might notice signs of manipulation when lies are involved. Family members with slight or severe Narcissism are the ones more prone to lying to you easily. You might notice when your family members are getting used to lying to you when your questions are met with vague answers. Additionally, you might also receive half-truths, which is essentially the same thing.

- Sometimes, family members end up giving you the silent treatment. One of the reasons why this technique works is because people eventually cave in. Those who have strong empathy are the ones who easily succumb to this tactic. If you have been a victim of this tactic, then you might have probably thought of swallowing your pride to initiate a conversation with the other person. When you budge and try to reconcile, you are not making the situation better. Rather, you are making it worse because you are basically letting the other person know that they can simply stay silent to control you.

- We are going to bring back gaslighting here because families are notorious for using this tactic. Family members are capable of gaslighting each other, trying to prove that the other person is either crazy or delusional. You might notice that every family has some element of this trait. The only difference is that in most families, it takes a mild form. In others, the intensity of gaslighting is ramped up to the point that one family member is taking advantage of the other.

- Family members use guilt trips to push you into a corner. Since family members are people you know intimately, guilt trips are extremely effective. Family members mostly make you feel guilty when you confront them about something.

- Often, your family members might resort to shaming your weaknesses or bring them repeatedly, especially during a confrontation. Shaming you is an effective way to make you feel vulnerable. Your vulnerability then makes you susceptible to manipulation.

So now that you are aware of the various techniques employed by family members to manipulate you, let's see how you can defend against them.

- The best way to stop the act of manipulation is to bring together the entire family and talk about positive communication. You don't have to single out the family member who is being manipulative. Simply talk about building trust and honest communication to everyone in the group.

- Take time out to think about the thoughts you have been thinking and the actions you have been performing. Are these thoughts and actions a result of your own will? Or did they happen because of a family member? Do you have your own beliefs with you or do you feel someone has injected a new belief system in you?

- Set boundaries between you and the family member who is being manipulative. This works best after going through the previous step of identifying yourself. You will know how much of your thoughts and actions are yours and how much was influenced. By identifying these faux thoughts and actions, you know exactly what kind of boundaries you should set with your family member; he or she has now become predictable.

- Don't always engage the Manipulator in his or her environment of choice. For example, if your sibling calls you over to their room to discuss something, ask them to meet in the living room instead (or any other room where people can easily walk into). This puts them off their game and gives both parties the power to communicate.

- Be patient. Do not rise to the bait. Give yourself time to react. When you know you are being manipulated, do not react instantly. When you receive the opportunity, set down a time to talk and explain the situation with the Manipulator. Once you have done that, give them the chance to make changes in their lives. If your family member truly values the family, then he or she won't have trouble mending their ways. If they continue being manipulative, then realize that you have tried everything and that you have a life to lead as well.

Love bombing is a form of emotional manipulation used by Manipulators to lower your defenses. It involves intense, abundant, and forceful display of positive emotions — especially love — towards the victim. Now you might find this rather odd. After all, if someone would like to manipulate the victim, then why would he or she show positive feelings or love?

According to psychologists (Degges-White, 2018), love bombing results in intense feelings of trust, love, and affection from the victim towards the Manipulator. This is exactly what the Manipulator is looking for. The extent to which the Manipulator uses love bombing — and who he or she uses it on — depends on the personal assessment of the Manipulator.

One of the things that makes love bombing dangerous is the fact that you cannot usually think of displays of love as negative. When someone showers you with love, you typically react positively. But that is exactly the reaction that the Manipulator expects from you.

Love bombing is a complex method of manipulating someone. The Manipulator must know exactly how much "love" to shower on someone. Certain people like honest compliments while others enjoy gifts.

This is why, if someone is attempting to use love bomb on you and they are not good at it, you can easily pick out their intentions. In fact, you might feel rather uncomfortable spending time with the person. In present parlance, one could say you might be "creeped out" in the presence of the Manipulator.

However, experienced Manipulators know exactly how much love to show a person. They understand how to slowly gain the confidence of someone and then strike when they get an opportunity.

There is a certain love bomb "litmus test" that you can use to see if the relationship you have entered is a result of love bomb or not.

Think of your best friend or someone you trust to a high degree. Think of the things that you and your friend have in common and all the things that you two like to agree or disagree about. Now realize the time it took to create that bond between you and your friend. Now compare that to your recent relationship. Do you think it is possible that someone you just met knows more about you than your best friend? If you feel that the person you met does seem to know you as well as your friend, then you should have alarm bells ringing in your head.

Additionally, you should also look for the following indications:

- Someone who is constantly trying to work with your ego.

- Try to push the relationship into areas that you are not comfortable with or ready for.

- Easily show warmth and affection to you, but cannot stand it when things do not go their way or if they are opposed.

But what can you do if you already find yourself in a situation with a Manipulator? Here are a few steps you can take:

- Do not be hesitant about setting boundaries in your relationship. Make sure that before you even take the relationship further, you have set milestones that help you take the relationship from one stage to another. If your partner is trying to rush the relationship, then you should beware of his or her intentions.

- If the relationship has already progressed farther than you had anticipated, then make sure you approach your family and friends for help.

- Unless you are absolutely certain, do not confide in the person your personal affairs. Furthermore, make sure that you are asking about his or her personal life in return. Try to see how comfortable he or she is when answering your questions. Usually, Manipulators are adept liars so there are chances that he or she might have a response for almost any question you pose. But with enough lies, you might be able to spot something odd in their story.

- Never show your emotions too easily to the Manipulator. Additionally, never show that you are interested in him or her. Try to make informed decisions about your relationship. Has he or she requested something from you that you typically do not give out in the initial stages of your relationship? Then make sure that you do not change that rule.

- If you need to put a hold on your relationship because you suspect the person of manipulating you, then you should do so. Let's say that you have been spending time with the individual every alternate day. Go ahead and avoid meeting for at least a week and see what happens. You might, of course, receive notes of concern, which is normal. But if you discover someone acting too normal or unconcerned, then you should be worried. In most cases, Psychopaths and Manipulators are so used to being in control, that they extend it towards their emotions as well. A sense of cold detachment is definitely a warning sign.

THE BEGINNING OF THE END

Much of what you see in CEM might not sound really frightening. but remember this: every manipulation has to start somewhere.

People cannot manipulate you entirely with a direct approach. They cannot simply make you do whatever you want without first gaining your trust, attention, and loyalty while also lowering your defenses.

All the techniques mentioned in this chapter are to help prevent you from falling deeper into the pit of manipulation. You can use them to avoid becoming a victim of Dark Psychology or encouraging manipulative actions from those close to you.

But now that we have touched on the ways manipulation can take place, it is time to head deeper into the pit to a place where you won't.

CHAPTER 4: UNDERSTANDING MIND GAMES

Most people think of mind games and mind control as something straight out of a science-fiction movie. People have this curiosity to find out what would happen if someone were to influence or control minds.

Typically, you might also find conspiracy theories about government-funded programs that apparently use human guinea pigs to test out some radical new mind control technique or device. While many of the mind control theories are false, a few might turn out to be more than just theories.

Take for example project MKUltra (History.com Editors, 2017), which was a top-secret project conducted by the CIA. The project involved hundreds of secret experiments on unsuspecting U.S. citizens to test the effects of drugs, such as LSD, for information gathering, mind control, and psychological torture.

Despite the fact that the project went on from 1953 to 1973, the project did not come to public attention until 1975. Even then, it occurred due to a congressional investigation into unauthorized — and potentially dangerous — experiments carried out by the CIA.

But why is there such a deep fascination for the powers of the mind and how to exploit them?

Perhaps one of the most important reasons is that the mind is such a complex part of the human experience. There are numerous ways one can use it to exploit others. This sense of control benefits those who seek to use mind manipulation and control techniques to achieve an end goal.

Because of this fascination with the mind, there have been numerous developments in the sphere of Dark Psychology.

We are now going to delve deeper into some techniques that are used to play mind games on unsuspecting victims.

BRAINWASHING

In the world of psychology, brainwashing is a process of thought reform that takes place through social influence. In psychology, social influence happens on a daily basis. You are constantly being influenced by numerous ideas, suggestions, and feedback that may change your beliefs, attitudes, or behaviors.

Social influence is very clandestine. You may not know that it occurs. In fact, the change in your behavior might feel so natural that you might just think that you have always been that way. There are numerous ways in which people can be affected by social influence.

You have the art of persuasion where someone or some idea is trying to convince you to act, think, or live in a particular manner because it could benefit you in a specific way. Then there is the education method, where you are told to do something because it is the right way of doing it. Everything from your table manners to the way you are supposed to tip cab drivers are all part of the education system.

Social influence by itself is not dangerous. In fact, it is an essential component of society. For example, someone who does not treat waiters or waitresses with respect might be told by his friends or colleagues that giving respect is the right thing to do. Eventually, that person might change his or her habits. But throughout the entire process, he or she might not be aware that they have been influenced. Their only recollection might be of their friends letting them know the right way to treat a waiter.

In similar ways, each country has its own cultural norms and traits. When people become aware of it, they change their attitudes and behaviors to become part of or move around harmoniously with that culture. In such instances, social influence is a benefit.

Brainwashing, on the other hand, is a severe form of social influence. It combines various aspects of social influence to change the way a person acts, thinks, or behaves, usually against the person's will or consent.

In order for brainwashing to work effectively, the victim needs to go through a state of complete dependency and isolation as the process is extremely invasive. It is for this reason that many cases of brainwashing occur in prison camps and totalitarian cults.

The Korean War gives us one example of brainwashing where American POWs were repeatedly subjected to brainwashing by their Chinese and Korean captors (Layton, 2006). The brainwashing was so potent that several POWs claimed to have arrived in the country for germ warfare (even though that was not the case). Many POWs also claimed allegiance to the nation of Korea and to Communism to such an extent that when they were eventually set free, they refused to return to the United States.

During brainwashing, the brainwasher has to gain complete control over the behavior of the victim. This means that he or she has to be able to control the sleeping and eating habits. Victims will eventually reach a point where they feel that all their needs can only be attended to by the brainwasher. The brainwasher then systematically begins to deconstruct the identity of the victim until it reaches a point where the victims cannot identify themselves anymore.

There are a few things to understand about brainwashing. Despite the fact that most psychologists are of the belief that brainwashing can be accomplished if the victim is subjected to the right conditions, there are some who are of the opinion that brainwashing cannot be accomplished to a severe degree. Regardless of what camp of belief you belong to, almost all psychologists agree that brainwashing does not completely destroy the personality of the individual. This means that while the victim might adopt a "new personality", the older personality is simply hiding. Psychologists agree that the effects of brainwashing are usually short-term. Victims can return to their previous selves if they can break free of the brainwasher.

It is for this reason, that most cults have their own location or space where they bring all the cult members together. By constantly keeping them in a location surrounded by brainwashing materials, the members do not receive an opportunity to think freely.

So how does brainwashing take place?

Well, modern psychologists arrange the entire process in three steps.

Step 1: Breaking Down the Self

This step focuses on breaking down the old identity of the victim. The agent performs this step so that the victim enters into a stage of vulnerability and acceptance, allowing for the introduction of a new identity. For the agent, this step could prove really challenging if the victim is firmly set in their old beliefs. For example, people who believe in religion might not easily give up on their beliefs for new ideas.

The agent uses numerous tactics to accomplish his or her mission. Let us look at what these tactics are.

Assault on Identity

The agent is going to use this tactic to systematically create havoc in the victim's sense of self, which includes the victim's ego, identity, and all their core beliefs. By doing so, the victim begins to feel that everything they believe in is wrong and they begin to question themselves. In this tactic, the agent is going to spend a fair bit of time trying to deny everything that the victim is.

If you take the example of prisoner camps, then the tormentors usually tell their victims something along the lines of, "You are not fighting for freedom or your country. You are simply being used by your government in a war that shouldn't be necessary."

Such phrases are used to instill a sense of doubt in the mind of the victim. It may not entirely bring down the victim's defenses, but it will definitely start making them question their beliefs.

Over time, the victims become disoriented, confused, and eventually, exhausted. Once they reach the point of exhaustion, their beliefs seem less concrete than before, giving way for the tormentor to take things further.

Guilt

Guilt is a difficult concept to grasp because it is a cocktail of emotions that make a person doubt his or her thoughts, actions, values, and beliefs.

According to the Carolina Partners in Mental Health (Greene, 2018), guilt includes several feelings including anxiety, shame, humiliation, and frustration. They further explain that guilt can eventually affect a person's self-esteem and self-worth.

For a tormentor or agent, guilt is a powerful weapon to use solely for the results it creates. He or she will constantly remind the victim of how terrible, wrong, or flawed their past personality was and why their new form is the one they should live with.

The agent will constantly attack the victim, reminding them of the small and big things of the past, to show how flawed their original personality was. Over time, the subject's sense of shame will make him or her susceptible to numerous suggestions.

Self-Betrayal

Making the victim feel bad about their past is just the first step. At any point, victims can realize that they have been forced to come to a conclusion about their previous identities. When that happens, victims can break free of the influence of the tormentor.

This is why, the agent will work to influence the victims to admit that not only were their previous selves the "bad" personality, but that they are willing to change.

At this point, it is important to remember that the victim is feeling extreme levels of shame, frustration, and disorientation. Tormentors can use a combination of psychological and physical attacks to break whatever defenses the victims are still holding on to. They will guide the victims to denounce their beliefs, family members, friends, or anything else that victims hold on to.

Breaking Point

In the final step, victims have lost all sense of their identity. They are going to experience an identity crisis and experience some severe symptoms that include deep depressions, severe sobbing, extreme anxiety, and other psychological attacks.

During this point, the agent will start laying down the groundwork for creating a new identity for the victim.

Step 2: Possibility of Salvation

In this step, the tormentor is going to offer salvation to the victim. At this point, the tormentor will show kindness, understanding, and a false sense of empathy. Victims are given the opportunity to see what is happening around them. They might even be shown certain luxuries, as an offering for their complete compliance.

This step takes place in four stages.

Leniency

The tormentors are going to approach the victims with false promises of help. They will talk to the victims as their friend, letting them know that everything they had been through was because the tormentor was simply trying to help them.

Because victims are feeling a deep sense of shame and guilt about their past lives, they are willing to take any release that is offered to them.

For example, tormentors might provide a delicious meal to the victims, showing them that they never wanted to hurt them in the first place. They even begin to ask a few personal questions about the family of victims, some of the things they enjoy doing, and so on. At the state that the victim is in, these little offerings of kindness might seem like a big deal. In some cases the tormentor might adjust the degree of kindness that he or she would like to show.

Let's take the example above. In certain cases, the tormentor might offer a nice meal but in other cases, he or she might actually set up a three course meal and perhaps even add a little music. Each of these things are made to show the victim that they were not manipulated with malice.

Compulsion to Confession

This step is almost similar to the "Self-Betrayal" stage in the previous step. At this point, the tormentor wants to extract a confession from the victim.

While the act of self-betrayal was focused on denouncing the previous identity, the Compulsion to Confession stage is related to getting the victim to admit that he or she is ready to take on a new identity. This stage is important because if the victim does not want the new identity, then he or she might feel that there is something not right about the new identity in the future.

At this point, if the brainwashing has been successful, then the victim might even reciprocate some of the kindness shown to them. They might respond to the attention shown to them by their tormentor.

Channeling of Guilt

When victims reach this stage, then they have been subjected to the brainwashing process for so long that they do not know the reasons behind their shame and guilt. Their mind has adopted their new identity. They are not able to clearly tell anyone what wrong they have committed. All they know is that they have committed something terrible and had to do something to right the wrong. In other words, all the guilt and shame has lost its meaning, even though they exist in the victims.

For the tormentor, this is an opportunity. At this point, he or she is going to create an explanation for the victims on the source of their guilt or shame. They can choose to alienate the victim from anything that they would like. Many tormentors create this impression that the old belief system that the victim had was corrupt.

Releasing of Guilt

When the victim reaches this point, they cannot bear to hold on to the guilt and shame. They want to rid the burden of such negative feelings. They are going through a period of psychological exhaustion where they simply want to look for clarity and a "normal" state of mind.

The tormentor on the other hand is holding on to the lifeline that will liberate the victim from all the discomfort they are feeling. The victims feel a sense of control at this point because the tormentors want the victims to feel like that are in control of their destiny. The tormentors are simply waiting for the transformation from the old identity to the new identity to become complete.

Step 3: Rebuilding of Self

At this point, the change is almost complete.

By this point, the victim has been put through so much emotional, psychological, and physical trauma that they cannot think beyond the trauma and examine their life. They are not capable of any coherent thought.

At this point, the victims cannot simply adapt to a new identity. They need to be guided into the process. The tormentors then become their mentors, letting them know the steps that they should take to complete the change.

Starting Over

Victims will now completely embrace their new identity. To many of these victims, they embrace the identity to such an extent that they begin to wonder why they had ever lived with their previous identity.

The victims feel that they have committed the change themselves, even though it was the work of the tormentors the whole time.

In some cases, if the victims begin to show signs or withdrawal or backtracking to their previous identity, then the tormentor subjects the victims to the entire process again. If required, the process will be repeated multiple times, until the tormentor has full control over the psychological and emotional states of the victim.

HYPNOSIS

While brainwashing is a common method of controlling and influencing the minds of victims, hypnosis is equally dangerous.

When one thinks of the word hypnosis, they imagine swinging pendulums and sinister individuals. In Dark Psychology, misuse of hypnosis can lead to dangerous results, but we will get to that in a moment. For now, we are going to understand how hypnosis is used to benefit us.

The Good

If you look through the information provided by WebMD (Bhandari, 2018), then in psychotherapy, hypnosis is used to help the patients enter into a state through guided relaxation, focused attention, and a heightened state of concentration.

Hypnosis is usually performed by a mental health specialist for mainly two reasons:

- Analysis: The specialist or therapist would like to get to the root of a particular psychological symptom or a specific problem. Sometimes, the patient finds it difficult to explain the problem or confess it openly. In such cases, hypnosis helps bring out the past trauma. The therapist usually does this after informing the patient about the process and does not use any clandestine techniques to achieve his or her goals.

- Suggestion therapy: In a hypnotic stage, people become more open to suggestions. When used for the right reasons, it can help people in many ways. Many people volunteer for hypnotherapy sessions to stop bad habits such as smoking, drinking, or even getting rid of certain fears. Therapists also use hypnotism to guide people through traumatic experiences and pain.

In fact, hypnotism moved from the occult and supernatural to science because of the 18th century German physician Franz Mesmer (Orne & Hammer, 2005). His main purpose for adopting hypnosis into his practice was to cure patients of certain maladies.

However, as the mind is complex, hypnosis can also be twisted for dark purposes.

The Bad

To understand how hypnosis can be used to harm a person, it is important to know just want happens during the process of hypnosis.

Simply put, different people experience hypnosis uniquely. Some patients under the influence of hypnosis claim that they feel a sense of deep relaxation and detachment. Others have reported that their actions seem to happen outside their direct influence. There are still others who are capable of remaining conscious during hypnosis and even carry out proper conversations.

When you understand the above experiences that people go through during hypnosis, then you might realize that they can be controlled or influenced in a number of ways.

Which is why, it is important to shed an accurate light on what hypnosis really is so that you are fully aware before going through the process. Most therapists have a lighthearted approach to the whole process, but here are some truths that you should know about.

- Hypnotism is not always a state of relaxation. It is an artificial method of accessing someone's REM state. In mammals and birds, the REM (or Rapid Eye Movement) stage is a phase of a person's sleep that is distinguished by the rapid movement of the eyes. In this phase, the person or creature experiences vivid dreams. If the therapist so chooses, then he or she can enter a REM stage violently.

- There are always side effects to hypnotism. When hypnotism is misused on patients, then the patients can feel uneasy and dizzy after a suggestion. Sometimes, they could end up having an unnerving experience because of the suggestions made by the therapist. People have been known to have panic attacks, anxiety, insomnia, nausea, uncontrolled weeping, confusion, distortions in the way one perceives their body or self, attention deficiency, and more.

- Some hypnotists often say that you will be aware of what happens to you at all times. That is not true. There are many incidences of people blacking out completely during a hypnosis process and waking up having no recollection of what happened to them (Riordan, 2016).

- It has been said that hypnotists cannot make people do anything against their will. That is not entirely true. Think of the incident in Italy where a cashier was hypnotized into handing over the money from the cash register (Miller, 2008). With the right training, people can be made to do things against their will, even if they think that they are prepared for anything that comes their way.

- No one's moral codes and standings can help them against certain suggestions made during hypnotism. But people's moral codes can be flexible, even if they believe otherwise. Sometimes, a little leeway is all the hypnotist needs to make some dangerous suggestions.

The Ugly

Want to know the ugly truth? Hypnosis can get very dark.

The process can be used to cause harm to someone, whether it is unintentionally or intentionally. Those hypnotists who have strong ethics follow certain rules that enable them to prevent abusing the power they have.

Here are some of the dark elements or results that are possible because of hypnosis.

- We all have the need to be in control of our lives. When we lose that control, we feel that we have experienced a sense of violation. Therapists have to be very particular about this when they are giving suggestions to their patients under hypnosis. They should not make any assumptions about what their client might or might not need. This might compel them to make suggestions that are not what their clients require. In the same way, you should make sure that you have chosen the right therapist and made your problem clear. Mention to the therapist what you intend to get out of the program and what you do not want.

- The intent of the therapist is important when it comes to helping their patients. It is not wise to mix personal opinions and feelings about people in a professional setting. But just like all humans, it is not uncommon for therapists to be affected by their ego. In such cases, the therapist can perform the session under a heavy influence of their ego. Make sure that you have done your research about the therapist well before you even think about approaching one.

- Some therapists have been known to create false and illusory memories in their patients. If you thought such a thing could not have happened in real life, then you are mistaken. In the mid-1990s, numerous reports surfaced about therapists subjecting their patients to false memory syndrome (The Editors of Encyclopedia Britannica, 2007). What the therapists did was instill false memories in their patients. In one such case, patients came out of their hypnosis session with memories of parental sexual abuse, when no such abuse was had ever taken place. As the reports of such abuse grew, the American Psychological Association (APA) began to recommend to the public that if they are looking for therapists, then they should be cautious about who they choose.

- According to the Academy of Finland, a person under hypnosis can be induced with hallucinations. The academy further found that with the right suggestion, the patient's perception, such as the experience of color, can also be altered (Suomen Akatemia, 2013). This further goes to show just how much influence hypnotists can have on the mind of a person.

DARK PERSUASION

Many people in society engage in the act of persuasion.

If you think about it, the politician who is seeking more votes is using a form of persuasion. Advertisers use their own form of persuasion to encourage you to buy their products. Even your friends or relatives use a mild form of persuasion to convince you about something.

Society is riddled with persuasion in different forms.

There is even a positive form of persuasion. When law enforcement officials convince a suicidal person from jumping over the ledge or when the government persuades residents of an area to improve the overall cleanliness of the location, then a form of positive influence is taking place.

So what does dark persuasion mean?

Enter the Dragon: The Dark Side of Persuasion

One of the main differences between positive and dark persuasion is the motive. In positive persuasion methods, the intent of the individual, group, or entity using the powers of persuasion are for a good cause. On the other hand, dark persuasion does not even have a moral motive.

Most of the times, the motive behind dark persuasion is amoral. This is because dark persuasion is mainly used to force a person to go against his or her self-interest. In other situations, dark persuasion is simply used because the one persuading is hungry for power. This hunger compels persuaders to try and affect the lives of people. In many cases, the persuader has a twisted sense of watching people suffer. He or she simply uses dark persuasion to cause harm; no other motive drives them.

Even the outcome derived from positive persuasion and dark persuasion differs vastly. In positive persuasion, one of three outcomes are derived:

- There is a benefit to the individual or group who is being persuaded.

- There is equal benefit to both the persuader and the individual or group being persuaded.

- A mutual benefit for the ones being persuaded and a third party. To understand this, think of the example where a suicidal person has been persuaded by the authorities to not end his or her life. By doing so, the authorities have not only helped the person, but also his or her family members.

On the other hand, let's see what is happening on the darker side of the spectrum and the outcomes that result from the process.

- The persuader always benefits from dark persuasion. They can gain benefit directly or by slowly convincing the person to carry out certain actions.

- The person being persuaded does not receive any benefit at all.

- Lastly, those who are adept in dark persuasion can not only gain from the process and inflict harm on the individual being persuaded, but they can also cause harm to others as well. Dark persuaders are not afraid of the collateral damage of their actions. In fact, some seem to take a twisted pleasure out of it.

So how can one use dark persuasion to get what they want?

The Long Con

One of the main reasons that people are able to resist dark persuasion is because if someone tries to persuade them of something too quickly, then they get frustrated. They can easily see through the persuasion that is taking place. The Long Con solves both these problems.

In The Long Con, the persuader takes his or her time getting to know the victim. They will carefully befriend the victim and make sure that the victim trusts them implicitly. They are in no hurry to get what they want. They have found their mark and they will use all their patience to make sure that they are successful.

Once the victim is ready psychologically and lowered their mental defenses, the persuader is ready to make their move. Initially, the persuader will start off by using small positive persuasions. Because the victim is receiving the benefits of persuasion, they don't mind going along with it. Through this process, the persuader achieves two things:

- The victim becomes accustomed to the persuasions to a point where they lower their defenses.

- The victim also makes a mental link between the persuader and positive outcomes. In their eyes, the persuader is a source of positivity.

Here is an example of how The Long Con can work. Let's say that someone has lost a family member or a close relative. The victim is in a state of mourning. At that time, the persuader arrives as a friend to comfort them. Over time, the persuader makes sure that the victim is being given attention and care. At this point, the persuader does not use any persuasion techniques, simply provides the victim with an abundance of kindness and patience.

Eventually, the persuader starts using positive persuasion, which makes the victim feel even better. he might even suggest that the victim should take care of their finances at this point. For that reason, perhaps a new bank account would seem wise, would it not? Unaware of the malice behind the persuader's words, the victim goes ahead and does what the persuader suggested.

After all, they have been supportive, haven't they? It is only right to trust them now.

After a while the persuader begins to use dark persuasion on the victim, perhaps suggesting that the best use of their new bank account would be to make an investment in an upcoming business venture. Time to become independent after all.

Once the victim takes out the money and hands it over to the persuader, that's when the truth is revealed. Because after the persuader receives the money, they are nowhere to be seen. It's like they did not exist at all.

In essence, this is the basis of how a con artist works. The word con artist is short for confidential artist and refers to a person who gains the confidence of the victim. When the victim is at the most vulnerable position, the con artist takes advantage of the situation.

State Transference

The word "state" here refers to the general mood and emotional level of the person. If two or more people's deeds, emotions, and words are aligned, then they have achieved a strong congruent state.

There is a concept called The Law of State Transference. According to this concept, one person can easily transfer a strong emotional suggestion or state to another person. This is a powerful concept used by a dark persuader.

But how does it work?

When someone gets started on the process of persuasion, then he or she has a low level of state transference. The persuader then has to improve this state. To accomplish that, the persuader will force their thoughts to reach the same level as that of the victim. In other words, if the victim is sad, then the persuader will also be sad. When the persuader does this, they create a connection with the victim on a subconscious level (and we know how powerful the subconscious can be).

This situation is called a "state match"; the state of the persuader matches the state of the victim.

From this point onwards, the persuader will slightly change their behavior and mood to test how much connection they have with the victim. For example, the persuader will slowly alter the tone and speed of their voice and see how the victim responds. If the victim also increases the tone and speed of their voice, then the victim has entered a state of compliance. The persuader has reached a level called a "hook point."

Once the "hook point" has been created, the persuader is now free to make whatever suggestion he or she wants.

THE POWER OF THE MIND

There are many questions about the human brain that are still left unanswered by psychologists and scientists. Even now, no one is entirely certain why we sleep and dream. There have been many theories, but when you take into account the REM stage of sleep, then none of the theories can explain the inclusion of the stage.

In a similar way, the mind is susceptible to numerous mental influences and control. Not everyone can be aware of the various ways people can influence the mind. You may think that someone is merely interacting with you when they have more ulterior motives to do what they do.

As the adage goes, "knowledge is power." This is why having the right set of knowledge about brainwashing, hypnotism, and dark persuasion will allow you to be more aware of your interactions.

Of course, there is another important subject to cover. Let us look at deception.

CHAPTER 5: THE ART OF DECEPTION

While it is true that deception is an important component of manipulation (and other forms of mental influence techniques), the fact that it can be used in other processes or by itself makes it important to study it by itself.

Deception shares its meaning with bluff, subterfuge, beguilement, and deceit. Together, they have slight variations but their end result is the same; they allow the agent to create beliefs in the victims that are either entirely false or half-truth.

Deception can include a lot of tactics including propaganda, distraction, sleight of hand, dissimulation, concealment, and camouflage. In order for the agent to completely control the mind of the subject, the subject has to enter into a state of trust. Once this is done, the subject will then believe the suggestions of the agent and even change their life and viewpoints in the future.

There are various types of deception that can take place. Let us look at them.

TYPES OF DECEPTION

Deception involves lies and deliberate omission of facts, in order to convince the subject of a particular viewpoint or reality.

There are 5 different types of deception, according to the Interpersonal Deception Theory (Hearn, 2006). Some of these types of deception are also found in other forms of mind control.

Lies

This is a common form of deception where the agent gives information that is completely different from the truth. When the agent presents the lie to the victim, it does not appear as a lie because of the level of trust that has been established between the agent and the victim. If the victim realized that the information provided to him or her was false, then they would not be talking to the agent and, therefore, not caught in the trap of deception.

Equivocations

When an agent of deception makes ambiguous, contradictory, or indirect statements, then he or she is providing equivocations. The agent intentionally does this in order to confuse the victim and ensure that they do not know what is happening to them or in that particular situation. It is also a defensive technique used by the agents. If the victim returns to them and blames them for spreading false information, the agent can deny the accusation completely, since they did not stick to one piece of information.

Concealments

Apart from lies, concealment is also one of the common types of deception that are used. In this process, the agent intentionally omits certain information that is important or relevant to the situation, discussion, or context. This way, the agent has not directly lied to the victim, but they have definitely withheld information, leading to confusion and errors in judgment.

Exaggeration

By using exaggeration, the agent will stretch the truth or overstate the facts in order to present the facts the way they would like or direct the course of events in a particular way. With exaggeration, the agent might not always lie to the victim, but the situation might seem more intense than it actually is.

Understatements

On the opposite side of an exaggerated statement, we have an understatement. Agents use this technique to lower the intensity or downplay the facts. Either way, the victim sometimes feels like he or she does not have to take any necessary actions when in fact, they need to attend to the situation immediately.

MOTIVATIONS FOR DECEPTION

So why do people deceive others? What drives them to compel someone else to diverge away from a particular direction, idea, information, or thought process?

Here are the six main reasons that agents use deception.

Preservation of Self-Image

A lot of times, the agent might feel that their self-image has come under threat. In such circumstances, the agent might use exaggeration to bolster the image he has placed in the minds of others. The agent might use concealment to mask certain information that could probably reveal some of his or her shady dealings.

What the agent is doing here is entering into a phase called "impression management." This is like the PR of a big company. When something attacks a company's image, then it is the PR's job to minimize the damage and preserve the company's reputation.

The same concept applies here, except that this time, we are focused on a single individual instead of a big company.

Personality Disorders

Sometimes, the ability to deceive and lie to people is born out of a much deeper problem. In this case, it could be because of *Narcissistic Personality Disorder* or due to *Machiavellianism.* In both cases, the person is trying to take advantage of the victim for a personal reason. Additionally, Psychopaths and Sadists can gaslight someone by using deception.

Pathological Lying

In many cases, the person has gotten so used to lying to the point where it is difficult for them to speak the truth. In such cases, the agents are deceiving out of sheer habit.

Boosting One's Reputation

With people such as Narcissists, using the ability of deception is one of the ways that they can ensure that they can boost their reputation. When they have to, they can exaggerate their accomplishments and lie about their failures. Narcissists can easily modify their stories to fit a certain narrative so that people can always view them as someone exceptional.

Conflict Evasion

Lies are often told to avoid conflicts. Typically, Machiavellians do not like to face conflict. One of the main reasons for this is that they like to be in control of the person and the situation. When conflicts arise, then everything they have set up to control their victims fail. To them, control is how they can get someone to do things for them.

Instant Gratification

If the very act of deception can bring instant rewards to the deceiver, then he or she may enjoy the very act of lying. Think about Sadists, who enjoy watching others suffer. If they can lie to someone and watch as the outcome causes hardships and pain, then they would very much like to deceive their victims as much as possible.

HOW TO SPOT A DECEPTION?

Difficult to Rely on Self

When people are honest, they are comfortable using the "I" pronoun. If a person who is guiltless is explaining his or her actions, then it might sound something like this: "I do not know how the stain appeared on the carpet. I was right here the whole time. In fact, I was watching a new episode of that TV show that they had going. You know the one about the town and creepy monsters."

On the other hand, when someone wants to deceive you, they use words and phrases that minimize any references to themselves.

So let us take the example above and see how a deceptive person is going to approach the scenario.

- Rather than "I do not know how the stain appeared on the carpet," the deceiver might say, "The stain was already there on the carpet."

- Rather than "In fact, I was watching a new episode of that TV show that they had going," a deceiver's response might be, "Well, they had that new TV show going on and it was an interesting watch."

Another telltale sign that someone is trying to deceive is by noticing the extra use of the "you" pronoun.

For example, they might say something along the lines of:

"You know, there was this TV show that was interesting. Did you see anyone else near the carpet? You could try asking John upstairs, he might know something."

Verb Tense

Honest people typically tend to describe events using the past tense. When someone is deceiving you, then they transform the past tense into the present. One of the main reasons for the change in the tense is because a deceiver is trying to recollect the events in their minds again and see how best to fabricate them. It is difficult to imagine the incident, edit it to suit a certain narrative, and at the same time focus on the tense.

Think of the above example, involving the stain on the carpet.

Typically, someone deceiving you would say:

"I was right here watching the TV. I *am* actually watching this cop drama, that seems fairly interesting and I *am* curious to see how it ends."

At that point, the person is either deceiving you or feels uncomfortable about something and is confabulating the story. At this point, it is better to find out for yourself.

Answering Questions With Questions

Sometimes, deceivers do not like to deceive because the probability of catching them in the act increases with each new deception. For that reason, they respond to questions with other questions. In numerous occasions, their questions tend to be either exaggerated or understated, depending on the scenario.

For example, they could exaggerate and say:

- "Why would I do that to my own family?"

- "Do you think that I, of all people, would do that?"

- "Where would you hear something like that?"

On the other hand, an understated question might be something like:

- "That's it? Why worry about something so trivial?"

- "Why do you think I would do that?" The deceiver asks this question while feigning nonchalance.

Not only are they trying to avoid answering the question directly, but they are trying to guide the conversation in a direction that they can control.

Euphemisms

Numerous languages around the world offer alternatives for a particular expression. This allows the sender of the message to tone down the intensity of the message to be conveyed.

For example, rather than simply saying, "My uncle died last year," which might be a bit too blunt, one could say, "My uncle passed away last year."

Or rather than saying, "You are dressed like a bum," you could perhaps tone it down to something more acceptable like, "Keep your outfit semi-casual. You look marvelous in it."

However, for deceivers, using euphemisms is to replace harsh words with milder ones as a way to portray their actions in a more favorable light. By avoiding the usage of explicit terms, the guilty party can make the harm look less impactful than it is.

When listening to a guilty party, look for words that sound less threatening. For example, they would rather use the word "missing" instead of "stolen" or "borrowed" instead of "took."

Let's say that you have a colleague who is quite deceptive and a Narcissist. He or she needs to exert control and show who's the boss in the office. Using passive-aggressive techniques, he or she lets you know that you should probably not try and take their chance at that promotion. Your colleague has taken an aggressive stance with a thin veneer of threat. You decide that the best course of action would be to inform your manager and let the manager decide the outcome of the situation. When the manager eventually calls you both to the office, your colleague, using euphemism, says, "I was simply *explaining* how important the promotion is. But I am not going to stand in the way of honest work. May the best man/women win."

By simply replacing the word "threat" with "explain," your colleague has turned himself from a dangerous coworker to an open and communicative individual, who respects hard work.

Oaths

Apart from giving as little information as possible, deceivers also tend to take many oaths. Words such as "Honestly," "I swear to God," "On my honor," are just some of the phrases that they use liberally in their conversation. This does not mean that honest people don't take oaths. To them, proving the truth is more important and only when they realize the situation is desperate, do they resort to oath-taking. Deceivers, on the other hand, are trying to hide the truth. They have to use anything else, other than actual proof, to explain their actions.

Allusion

Deceivers try not to admit to taking or not taking a particular action. They simply allude to an action.

Let us take the example of the stain on the carpet. A deceiver who wants to avoid the truth resorts to allusion by saying:

"I usually try not to walk a lot on the carpet. Most of the time, I make sure that I sit and watch the TV. I wanted to ask John about the stain."

Did they or did they not walk on the carpet? Were they sitting in front of the TV the whole time? Did the individual even attempt to ask John about the stain?

Nothing is clear with the deceiver. Everything they say seems to hint at a particular action, but never really makes any connection between the action and the deceiver.

Lack of Details

When people tell the truth, they try to pack in as much detail as possible. This is because they are trying to give you specific details that you could check to corroborate the truth. Even if they have a hard time adding details, they try to throw in as much information as possible; the music playing in the restaurant, the color of their shirt, a fancy car that they remember during the course of the evening, or even the food they ate and the prices on the menu. They will supply you with anything to make sure that you are convinced that they are telling the truth.

With deceivers, everything is vague. Their statements are very simple because they are fabricating a story. In a false story, adding details is not only difficult but dangerous to the deceiver as well. If they add in a detail and you go ahead to check the authenticity of that detail, then their lies might be exposed.

CHAPTER 6: DARK PSYCHOLOGY JUJUTSU: PROTECTING YOUR MIND

Let's face it; simply going around being cautious of every single person that you meet is going to be really stressful. You might get so obsessed with finding a Psychopath, that you might just end up looking or acting like one. To avoid such social awkwardness and unpleasantries, there are a few things you can do to train your mind to be strong and receptive to mental manipulations, tricks, and deception.

The first thing that you have to remember is that we are all emotional beings. As we saw earlier in this book, our subconscious mind is equally — if not more — powerful than our conscious mind. This means that sometimes, we feel a surge of emotions when we least expect it. Have you ever heard your favorite music and felt something? Have you ever stepped into the midst of nature and felt a sense of relief or calmness? Have you enjoyed delicious food or felt excitement when you bought something you have wanted to buy for a long time?

In many cases, our emotions just make us who we are. And in all honesty, we should not change that.

However, there are certain things that you can do to ensure that you are not a victim of manipulation.

We are going to look at two ways to avoid being the victim of mental games or manipulations. The first thing that you are going to do is become emotionally strong.

Based on psychological recommendations, here are 7 ways for you to be mentally strong:

Identify Your Current Position

We all go through different phases in our lives. There is nothing wrong in feeling an overwhelming sense of sadness during a tragedy or joy when you receive something. But make sure that you are aware of what is happening around you. This is particularly true when you are feeling emotionally exhausted or you are experiencing a sense of disconnection from certain aspects of your life.

Take a Break

Never be afraid to get away from things that can get too overwhelming in your life. Sometimes, it is better to take a vacation so that things can settle down and you can probably figure out what you are going through. These breaks also help you figure what course of action you would like to take in your life.

Calm Yourself

Never be hesitant to take on some self-soothing techniques. These help you out in a jam. When you begin practicing these techniques, you might have to pay attention to the technique as you perform it. Eventually, you will train your subconscious to prime these techniques automatically when you need them.

Have you ever been in a situation where you are so used to waking up at a particular time in the morning that, even without an alarm, your body just pulls you out of sleep at that particular time or close to that time? The same concept applies here.

Once you train your mind enough, your calming techniques kick start automatically when you need them.

Counseling

If you feel like you require some sort of counseling, make sure that you get it. The best way to improve is to admit that there are areas that need to be improved. Then go about systematically improving each area until you feel more confident about managing them by yourself.

Engage in Physical Activities

Work the body and you can work the mind. Try and engage in whatever physical activity you are able to, even if it involves just walking around your neighborhood or performing a few sets of push-ups at home.

Denial

Do not deny that you are going through an emotional period in your life or that you are capable of showing certain emotions during certain moments. Do you get upset easily? Do you get sad by seeing the plight of animals? Does indulging in your favorite hobby bring you a lot of joy? When you can identify yourself as a person, then you are better aware of who you are. This way, nobody else can claim to know you better than you do yourself or try to use tactics to convince you of something you are not certain about.

Create Goals

When you have certain goals to work towards, you won't let anyone distract you with emotions. Even if you were to engage in romantic or sexual relationships, you are going to be more aware of what is going on around you. This is because your main priority is not the relationship itself. You are not in a desperate frame of mind to find some sort of connection with someone or need someone else to guide your life. You know what you have to do and you are going to do it by yourself.

MENTAL TECHNIQUES

The above techniques are simple measures that you can implement in your daily life. But we need to make sure that you are working on strengthening your mind by using specific psychological techniques.

We are not only going to look at ways to avoid mental manipulation but also how to stop them if you think you are already being manipulated by someone.

So let us get started.

Know Your Human Rights

The first thing that you are going to do is learn, memorize, and understand your human rights. Most people think that they shouldn't do something because it is inappropriate or considered rude. They are unsure where to draw the line and how much tolerance they should give a person who seems to be constantly encroaching within personal boundaries.

These are the rights that you should always keep in mind, especially when you are interacting with strangers or acquaintances:

- You are a unique individual who deserves the right to be treated with respect.

- You have the right and freedom to express your wants, opinions, and feelings. If you prefer to withhold certain emotions, you are doing so because you want to, not because someone told or convinced you to.

- You have the right to establish and follow your own set of rules and priorities.

- You are allowed to say "no", without feeling pressured not to.

- You deserve to receive what you paid for.

- You can have different views and opinions than others.

- You have every right to take care of your physical, psychological, and emotional states and to defend yourself against physical, psychological, and emotional attacks.

- You have the freedom and right to create a life filled with happiness and good health.

Understand the Dark Side of Human Psychology

Make sure that you glean as much information as possible about the dark side of psychology from this book and use it in real life. If you feel that something is off about a particular person, even if that person happens to be your friend or family member, then make sure you examine the situation and the person. Do not hesitate to use the points mentioned in this book for your own analysis of the person. Remember that you are not doing it to cause harm to anyone, but rather to see if you are about to be mentally manipulated.

Start Taking Notes on What People Say During Conversations

If you feel like someone said something that seemed rather odd, then make sure that you note down what they said. Try to add in as much detail as possible. For example, what was the context of the conversation? Did you notice anything else about the person when he or she made the odd remark? Is this the first time you are meeting this person? Can you remember how you responded?

Note taking helps you analyze the situation from a third-person perspective. Many times, you might feel that you have made a mistake during the conversation. But after you analyze your notes, you might just realize you were being manipulated all along.

Furthermore, when you have taken down notes, you can refer to it later whenever you want to. This becomes important when Manipulators deny saying something that they had previously said. If you notice someone denying their remarks, then you know that there are chances of an emotional manipulation about to occur in your life.

Avoid Emotional Attachments With Manipulators

When you have identified a Manipulator, make sure that you avoid all emotional attachments to them. This way, they won't have any leverage on you and you won't inadvertently divulge something that you are not supposed to.

While you are at it, try and reveal as little emotion as possible. Do not give them something that they can use as pressure points or hook points in the future. We have already discussed what hook points are. Pressure points, on the other hand, refer to certain actions or words that can elicit an emotional response from you. Do not give away the keys to your emotions that easily.

Prime Your Mind

One of the best ways to keep your awareness ready is to prime your subconscious. By reading this book and by gaining a deep sense of understanding about yourself, you will be able to start fueling your subconscious with ideas about emotional manipulation. The more you feed your subconscious, the more prepared and aware it becomes.

Avoid Blaming Yourself And Taking Things Personally

Remember that you are not in the wrong here. At any point in time, do not start thinking that you have done something wrong. Your best weapon is your will. No matter what techniques the Manipulator uses, if you ever feel like doubting your actions or blaming yourself for something, take a break. Do not meet with the person and begin analyzing your actions. If you start noticing signs that the person has made you feel guilty about something you were not even responsible for or cannot be blamed for, then you have to approach the person in a new light.

Here are some questions you can ask yourself whenever you are about to blame yourself:

- Was I or am I treated with the respect that I deserve? More importantly, is the respect shown to be genuine?

- Would I consider the person's expectations of me reasonable?

- Is one person (me) giving too much in this relationship? Has the other person contributed to the relationship?

- Finally, do I feel comfortable and happy in this relationship? Do I sometimes have the feeling that something is wrong?

Shift Focus

If you feel that you are constantly under the spotlight, then make sure that you confidently shift the focus back to them. Do not be afraid to ask probing questions about them and their life.

Whenever you hear a request or demand, do not be afraid to ask the Manipulator questions about it. Put the focus on the Manipulator so that you are making them aware of their actions.

Here are some examples of questions that you can use:

- Do you think that what you have asked me is reasonable?

- Do I get to speak my opinion on this?

- Are you asking me to do it or telling me to?

- Are you really asking me to (repeat the unreasonable request)?

- Shouldn't I get a say in this as well?

Use The Long Con to Your Advantage

Some Manipulators can take their time to work on your emotions. Make sure that you are using time to your advantage as well. If someone requests or demands something from you, feel free to say, "I'll think about it" or "Let me see if I have the time for it."

Don't be eager to jump to conclusions. Take your time to evaluate the situation and consider the pros and cons.

CONCLUSION

The mind is a complex region.

You are going through so many experiences every day that your mind is constantly learning new things and absorbing new information, habits, and traits. But at the end of it all, you are the master of your mind.

Do not hand over the dominion of your mental faculties, capabilities, and areas over to anyone. Those who truly care about you and love would not insist on making you say or do anything that you do not like.

Remember that a healthy dose of skepticism is always welcome. It does not make you an irrational person or a pessimist. Trying to question something does not place you under the banner of "bad," "wrong," "despicable," or any other negative connotations. You are simply using the power of rational thought to decide for yourself where a situation is going and what you are going to do about it.

Finally, Dark Psychology is real.

Do not let Manipulators work the situation against you.

You work the situation against your Manipulators.

Dark Psychology Secrets Revealed

Mind The Gap Between Perception and Reality

Thank you for reading this book.

If you found this book useful in any way, a review on Amazon is always
appreciated!

Mark Temple

9 781686 829598